H23 362 725 8

Please renew/return this item by the last date shown.

So that your telephone call is charged at local rate,
please call the numbers as set out below:

	From Area codes 01923 or 0208:	From the rest of Herts:
Renewals:	01923 471373	01438 737373
Enquiries:	01923 471333	01438 737333
Minicom:	01923 471599	01438 737599

L32b

17

6th June

2 7 MAR 2003

11/11

L 33

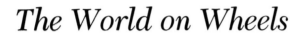

The World on Wheels

The World on Wheels

An Illustrated History of
the Bicycle and Its
Relatives

RUTH CALIF

New York • CORNWALL BOOKS • London

Cornwall Books
4 Cornwall Drive
East Brunswick, N.J. 08816

Cornwall Books
27 Chancery Lane
London WC2A 1NF, England

Cornwall Books
Toronto M5E 1A7, Canada

Library of Congress Cataloging in Publication Data

Calif, Ruth.
   The world on wheels.

   Includes bibliographical references and index.
   1. Bicycles—History.   2. Motorcycles—History.
I. Title.
TL400.C26   629.2′272′09   80-70511
ISBN 0-8453-4710-1   AACR2

Printed in the United States of America

Contents

Acknowledgments

The illustrations from *Scientific American* are reprinted by permission.

Chapter 12, "Pioneer Tourist," originally appeared in *Wide World*, American edition, published by the International News Company, under the title "Across America by Motor-Cycle."

Albert Van Buren of Yonkers, New York, supplied material about Augusta and Adeline Van Buren for chapter 22, "Women's Lib on Motorcycles."

The World on Wheels

1

Velocipede Mania

THE BICYCLE, FIRST CALLED A VELOCIPEDE, took Paris by storm before it crossed the Atlantic to America. Although velocipedes had existed since the 1700s, they did not become popular here until 1869. Then, like a fast-growing mushroom, they swept the country into faster locomotion than had been known. Because the demand for the vehicle was so great, bicycle manufacturers sprang up overnight, but were unable to make the machines fast enough for the demand.

By early 1869 the velocipede had conquered the entire world. San Francisco had entered the competition, producing improvements reflecting credit on its inventors. The Shanghai *News-Letter* stated that velocipedes had ceased to be novelties in the streets of that city, and that even the untaught Chinese ponies had become so used to them that they were no longer frightened.

The Japan *Gazette*, published in Yokohama, stated that a gentleman well known in that settlement took a trip to Yeddo on a velocipede and returned in safety. It further added that many persons had sent home for these locomotives, and some were on the way. Civilization no longer advanced solely with the locomotive and telegraph. It had called the velocipede to its assistance.

In *Howitt's Visits to Remarkable Places*, pub-lished in 1841, a description of a velocipede seen by the author during a visit to Alnwick Castle, North-umberland, England, was given.

Among the curiosities laid up here are also two velocipedes—machines which, twenty years ago, were for a short period much in vogue. One young man of my acquaintance rode on one of these wooden horses all the way from London to Falkirk, in Scotland, and was requested at vari-ous towns to exhibit his management of it to the ladies and gentlemen of the place. He afterwards made a long excursion to France upon it. He was a very adroit velocipedian, and was always very much amused with the circumstance of a gentle-man meeting him on the highway by the river side, who, requesting to be allowed to try it, and being shown how he must turn the handle in order to guide it, set off with great spirit, but turning the handle the wrong way, soon found himself hurrying to the edge of the river, where, in his flurry, instead of turning the handle the other way, he began lustily shouting "woh! woh!" and so crying plunged headlong into the stream. The Duke's horse, which is laid up here for the gratification of posterity, was, I believe, not so very unruly; yet I was told its pranks caused it to be disused and here stabled. It is said that the duke and his physicians used to amuse themselves with careening about the grounds on these steeds; but one day, being somewhere on the terrace, his grace's Trojan steed capsized, much to the amusement of a troop of urchins who were mounted on a wall by the road to witness this novel kind of racing. On this accident the velocipede was laid up in lavender, and a fine specimen of the breed it is.

In 1868 the Hanlon Brothers of New York patented a machine that foreshadowed the modern bicycle. It had only two wheels, the vehicle being kept in upright position while in motion by the skill of the rider. The power for propulsion was applied by the feet and the vehicle was steered by a lever worked by the hands, which was attached to the forked support of the forward wheel. The subjects of the Hanlons' patents were extension or adjustable cranks to suit the driver's peculiarities, an extension seat, and its adaptation for the use of ladies by means of an attachment similar to a sidesaddle. The vehicle could have three wheels—a steering wheel in front and two supporting wheels in the rear of the occupant—and in this form was better adapted to the use of women and children and to beginners. The seat in this improved velocipede was a spring, being supported on flexible steel or wooden strips and insuring ease of motion. The Hanlon Brothers exhibited this vehicle many times, and their evolutions rivaled in grace and rapidity those of the best skaters.

The *Scientific American*, a prestigious publication of the time, said, "For ease of motion and grace of action the velocipede ranks with the skate, with this advantage, however, that the former may be used at all seasons, instead of being restricted to periods of freezing temperature. Like every other machine which we have copied from other peoples, this has been materially improved by American mechanics."

The *Scientific American* was right. Over the next few years inventors vied with each other to improve and enhance the bicycle, and many in number were the inventions they patented. Some were practical, some ridiculous, but all were interesting.

It was agreed that the velocipede was destined to become a fixed fact as much as locomotives and steamboats, but the bicycle as we know it today had not yet been born. In the next quarter century, however, it would emerge as one of the main modes of transportation of the American people and assume much the same shape as it has today.

Hanlons' Patent-Improved Velocipede (Scientific American, 8/19/68)

Meanwhile, in 1869, the *Sun*, rival of *Scientific American*, was rather severe with some of the weird new contraptions being offered. "Before inventing a new velocipede, it would be advisable to become expert in riding those now in existence. Generally, our inventors have proceeded upon abstract principles, and have fallen into absurdities from which a little previous practical knowledge would have saved them." They went on to tell of an inventor who could rise the known velocipede, but his own device threw him, although it later proved to be of value.

The *Sun* wasn't negative about every invention, only about the bizarre. "We hear of novelties that are not without promise, and little additions to the comfort of riders are constantly made by manufacturers. One of the most valuable of these is the triangular movable pedal of Pickering, with which the feet can never be placed amiss upon the cranks."

The debate between the two publications continued as the *Sun* criticized the one-wheeled velocipede, an English invention, as being liable to give its riders broken noses. The *Scientific American* replied, asking, "Is it not probable that many of the devices which now meet the *Sun*'s disapprobation may turn out to be just the thing after all? Feats of balance are performed on equally as unstable a basis as this contrivance appears. Would it be

Rider on Unicycle (Scientific American, *2/13/69*)

more difficult to keep upright upon such a wheel, than to sit in a chair balanced upon two legs, resting upon the rather uncertain substratum of a slack rope?"

In the one-wheeler, the feet were placed on short stilts connected with the cranks, one on either side of the rim, while the rider sat upon a steel-spring saddle over the center of the whole wheel. The inventor modestly limited the diameter of the wheel to twelve feet, and the number of revolutions at fifty per minute. Twenty-five miles per hour was the speed expected to be reached.

It was a machine for daredevils, to be sure, but the two-wheeler was almost as dangerous for beginners. However, people really wanted to learn to ride this new conveyance, so the demand was met. Riding schools sprang up like mushrooms.

The *Times* took a velocipede census of New York and announced there were 5,000 pupils in various stages of advancement toward mastering the vehicle. "The rooms of the numerous velocipede schools are open almost, like the restaurants, 'at all hours,' but still disappointed applicants for admis-

sion have to be turned away. The greatest difficulty is, however, to get the velocipedes, the demand being far ahead of the supply."

Philadelphia had recently produced a velocipede of an entirely new style. It was two-wheeled, the seat low between the wheels, but its novelty was a cog attached to the guiding post, by means of which the rear wheel was made to follow in the track of the forward wheel. No matter how short the turn, both wheels made it at the same time, and the seat always remained parallel with the driving wheel. In other machines there was no guide to the rear wheel, and consequently the machine could not be turned readily when a collision threatened.

The *Evening Post* reported:

The velocipede fever continues to create excitement in Chicago. Two riding schools for instruction in the art of balancing upon these vehicles have been established, and the machines are kept for sale at various places. Its perfectly level streets—many of them paved with wooden blocks—are admirably suited to this species of propulsion, and several of its business men, living two or three miles from their offices, make their daily trips with two-wheeled vehicles, quickly leaving the discomfited horse-car men in the distance. The demand for velocipedes greatly exceeds the supply, and the smaller cities around are taking the contagion and sending in their orders. The lucky manufacturers must be reaping a rich harvest, and ought to reduce the present extortionate price of $100 and $125, as they doubtless will have to do eventually. Meantime Chicago hails any invention of a *fast* machine, and the velocipede is likely to become a practical institution there.

Velocipede races were commonplace, stage shows of riding feats enthusiastically attended, and "velocipede mania" ran rampant. The machine was a toy to some, an instrument of pleasure to others, and of great use to many.

Rural districts caught the mania, although machines were practically nonexistent. A velocipede school was established in Bridgeport, Connecticut, but one wag reported, "The nearest approach to a velocipede that has been seen in Danbury was a bit of orange peel, on which a citizen went across a sidewalk and down a pair of stairs in just 1¼ seconds—the quickest time on record."

From the beginning, pedestrians and cyclists

were at odds with each other. The *Sun* advocated an elevated railway from Harlem to the Battery, to be used only by the riders of velocipedes. "By this means it would be possible to go from one end of Manhattan Island to the other in about an hour, making allowance for delays from stoppage and accidents. A good rider, with a clear track, would easily accomplish the distance in half an hour."

They added, "By all means let us have the 'elevated roadway,' and let the sidewalks be kept clear for pedestrians, who are otherwise likely to be endangered by the carelessness or awkwardness of velocipedists."

The park commissioners prohibited velocipedes in the parks at first, the reason given that they would frighten the horses. They soon changed their tune, however, when public opinion prophesied a future population mounted on rolling stock that required no oats. By the summer of 1869 parks were catering to the velocipede with special roads and planned races.

A paper, *The Velocipedist*, was published the same year in New York. It had eight pages devoted to velocipede news, was published monthly in Pickering & Davis on Greene Street, and was another strong indication that the bicycle was here to stay.

Other newspapers reported the newest inventions, races scheduled, and had a rash of cartoons including the officials of the day in conjunction with a velocipede, usually in some outlandish catastrophe. *Harper's Weekly* even had the New Year coming in on a velocipede.

The career of the "Velocipedestrian" was not one of unalloyed happiness. Newspaper columinists answered such grave questions as:

> If a fellow goes with his velocipede to call upon a lady whose house has no front yard and no back yard, and there are boys in front of it ready to pounce upon his machine, and the lady is smiling through the window, what is he to do?
>
> If a fellow, riding his velocipede, meets a lady on a particularly rough bit of road where it requires both hands to steer, is he positively required to let go with one hand to lift his hat?
>
> If a fellow, riding his machine, meets three ladies walking abreast, opposite a particularly tall curb stone, what ought he to do?
>
> If a lady meets a fellow riding his machine, and asks him to go shopping with her, what can he do with the machine?
>
> If the hind wheel of a fellow's machine flings

mud just above the saddle, ought he to call on people who do not keep a duplex mirror and a clothes brush in the front hall?

> If a fellow is invited to join a funeral procession, ought he to ride his machine?
>
> If people, coming suddenly round corners, will run against a fellow's machine, is he bound to stop and apologize, or are they?
>
> Is it proper to ride a velocipede to church? If so, what should be done with the machine when a fellow gets there?

Even the poets got into the act. In 1869, the *New York Sun* printed the following:

Hans Breitmann's Shtory Apout Schnitzerl's Philosopede

Herr Schnitzerl make a philosopede
    Von of de newest kind;
It vent mitout a vheel in front,
    And hadn't none pehind.
Von vheel was in de mittle, dough,
    And it vent as sure as ecks,
For he shtraddled on de axel dree
    Mit der vheel petween his lecks.

Und ven he vant to shtart id off
    He paddlet mit his veet,
Und soon he cot to go so vast
    Dat every dings he peat.
He run her out on Broader shtreet,
    He shkeeted like de vind,
Hel! how he bassed de vancy craps,
    And lef dem all pehind!

De vellers mit de trotting nags
    Pooled oop to see him bass;
De Deutschers all erstaunished saldt:
    "Potztausend! Was ist das?"
Boot vaster shtill der Schnitzerl flewed
    On—mit a ghastly smile:
He tidn't tooch de dirt, py shings!
    Not vonce in half a mile.

Oh, vot ish all dis eartly pliss?
    Oh, vot ish man's soocksess?
Oh, vot ish various kinds of dings?
    Und vot ish hobbiness?
Ve find a pank note in de shtreedt,
    Next tings der pankish preak;

Ve folls, und knocks our outsides in,
  Ven ve a ten shtrike make.

So vas it mit der Schnitzerlein
  On his philosopede;
His feet both shlipped outsideward shoost
  Vhen at his extra shpede,
He felled oopon der vheel of coorse;
  De vheel like blitzen flew;
Und Schnitzerl he vos schnitz in vact
  For id shlished him grod in two.

Und as for his philosopede,
  Id cot so shkared, men say,
It pounded onward till it vent
  Ganz teufelwards afay.
Boot vhere ish now der Schnitzerl's soul?
  Vhere does his shpirit pide?
In Himmel troo de endless plue,
  It takes a meteor ride.

Perhaps the poem was written in dialect so as not to offend the delicate sensibilities of the ladies, but whatever the reason, its hilarity was unmistakable.

In the 1700s, Webster's definition of a velocipede was "a carriage for one person, having two wheels placed one before the other, in the same line, and connected by a beam, on which the person sits astride, and propels the vehicle by striking the tips of the toes against the earth."

By the 1800s that style was still in use to some extent in Paris, and was claimed to be equal in many respects to the new kinds generally in use, which were propelled by the foot and crank, or hand and lever. The old ones were more easily controlled, but the degree of speed could not be attained by striking the toes against the ground that was achieved by the crank movement.

As early as 1822, a London paper printed the following item:

A man upon a new sort of velocipede attracted a number of people together at the Elephant and Castle, London, on Thursday, to witness his activity and the swiftness with which he travels. He is a shoemaker by trade, and finding the trade bad at Newark-on-Trent, in Nottinghamshire, of which place he is a native, he built this mechanical horse, as he terms it. It is on a different plan from the others. It is worked by two handles, which set two wheels in motion, and cause two levers in front to be put in motion, which set the

machine going at the rate of at least six miles an hour. It is the completest machine of the kind that has as yet been invented. He has traveled in fine weather sixty miles a day. He has two iron stirrups in which he places his feet; and they keep him steady on the saddle.

To a population used to the horse for transportation, it was only natural that the first velocipedes somewhat resembled this animal. As late as 1862, models of horses were mounted on wheels.

P.W. MacKenzie, a citizen of the United States, patented a "cantering propeller," which was a

A "Cantering Propeller" (Scientific American, 3/20/69)

hobbyhorse mounted on wheels. It resembled the early ones, but he claimed a patent on the basis of improvements, as follows:

I claim, in combination with a saddle seat for the rider, the employment and use of a cranked axle, arms, and footrest, so arranged that power applied by the feet of the rider shall give motion to the vehicle, substantially as described and specified.

2. The combination of the following elements, namely, a saddle-seat for the rider, a cranked axle for propelling the vehicle by power applied by the feet of the rider, and a steering mechanism, so constructed that the direction of

travel of the vehicle may be governed by the rider, substantially as described and specified.

3. The universal joint, in combination with the fulcrum of the vehicle and the steering wheel, constructed and operating substantially as and for the purposes specified.

4. The hinged legs in combination with the body of the horse, and with the cranks, substantially as and for the purposes specified.

5. The foot-rests upon the arms, substantially as and for the purposes specified.

6. The double-armed levers and diagonal cords in combination with the handle and steering wheel, substantially as described and specified.

The first and second claims were intended to embrace the essential elements of the velocipede then in use, but it remained for the courts to determine whether the claims clashed.

The itch for wheels has been worldwide for quite a while. The first patent in this country was granted in 1818 to W. Clarkson, Jr., but when the Patent Office burned in 1836, the model and records were destroyed.

In a small New England village, about 1823, a Yankee boy was seen tearing around on a velocipede of his own construction, to the astonishment of the villagers and his great satisfaction. The "machine" was rudely constructed, the wheels being of boards nailed together crisscross, and the frame of such stuff as a farmer's woodpile could furnish, but it would "go like fun!" It was propelled by the *toes* (not the flat feet) lightly touching the ground.

The germ of the velocipede arose in the eighteenth century when a strange device called a "hobbyhorse" was introduced. It consisted of two wheels connected tandem by a rigid frame of wood. The rider sat on a saddle midway between the wheels and propelled it by means of strides on the ground. Its motion was limited to a straight line, but this rigid, nonsteering bicycle was the first step toward the modern machine.

The second step was taken in 1818, when Baron von Drais introduced a vehicle called a "draisienne," which resembled the hobbyhorse except that the front wheel was so arranged that steering was possible. Lewis Gompertz of Surrey in England made improvements that brought the arms of the rider into action to assist his legs. On the sketch, a handle (C) was worked backward and

1823 Yankee Boy Invention (Scientific American, 3/27/69)

forward. It was attached to a circular rack (DG), which worked in a pinion (E) with ratch wheel on the front wheel of the velocipede, and which, on being pulled by the rider with both hands sent the machine forward. When thrust from him, it didn't send it back again because of the ratch which allowed the pinion to turn in that direction free of the wheel.

H was the saddle, and B was made so the breast of the rider leaned against it while the sides came around him at some distance below the arms, and was stuffed. The rider could either propel the machine entirely with his arms, or he could use his feet.

The beam (A) was made of beech wood, and a pivot at F allowed the front wheel to be turned to the right or left at the will of the rider. Although somewhat clumsily shaped, it was quite an efficient machine for the times.

Such a cumbersome means of locomotion soon fell into disuse, and for a long time no real progress was made. Various systems and devices were introduced to enable the rider to propel himself, but they were mostly tricycles and still cumbersome and unmechanical.

The third step was the invention of the bicycle, an idea credited to a Scotchman, Gavin Dalzell. The motion of the pedals was downward, the feet describing a small segment of a circle. This motion

Arm and Leg Action Velocipede (Scientific American, *2/13/69*)

half several thousand francs were collected from cyclists, manufacturers, and friends of the enterprise.

Le Petit Journal had praised the once-scorned bicycle since 1891, bringing it back to a popularity unimagined in its early days. With everybody's approval, a statue was commissioned to honor the brothers, and since Pierre was born in Bar-le-Duc,

The Monument to the Michaux Brothers (Scientific American, *11/10/94*)

The Monument Erected at Bar-le-Duc in Honor of the Michaux Brothers Inventors of the Bicycle Pedal (Scientific American, *11/10/94*)

was transmitted to a crank attached to the axle of the rear wheel by levers. For a long time it was supposed that this invention dated from 1834, but in 1892 a close scrutiny of the matter resulted in the downfall of the legend, as a blacksmith's bill for the iron work was found, which proved that it was made in 1847, and also that another Scotchman, named MacMillan, had anticipated Dalzell's invention.

Pierre and Ernest Michaux, young French locksmiths, took the next great step which made the modern bicycle possible. In 1855, while repairing a draisienne, Ernest (fourteen years of age at the time) conceived the idea of applying cranks directly to the front wheel. He tried the device for a couple of days and then showed the machine to his friends.

Bicycles then had considerable success in the last years of the Empire, but the war ruined the Michaux brothers. France took little interest in the development of cycling until 1880, when the safety bicycle was put on the market.

The pedaled driving mechanism was improved by Pierre Lallement, to whom the credit of the invention is sometimes given, but the French knew the Michaux brothers had been first with the idea. In 1892 a committee was formed with M. Pierre Giffard as chairman, to honor the memory of Pierre and Ernest Michaux, who were looked upon as the real initiators of the bicycle pedal. In a year and a

it was decided to erect the monument at the intersection of two streets in that city. The architectural background for the work was designed by M. Demoget, while the charming bronze figure was a work by the sculptor Houssin. The inauguration of the monument took place on Sunday, September 30, 1894.

In 1869 a Parisian named Magee further improved the velocipede by making it entirely of iron

Pickering Velocipede (Scientific American, *1869*)

and steel. In the same year rubber tires were used. In 1869 Michaux conceived the idea of making the front or drive wheel larger than the rear wheel, and various other improvements—such as brakes— were introduced.

By this time machines were being constructed on both sides of the Atlantic Ocean. T. R. Pickering, of New York, designed a model, which his firm, Pickering and Davis, 144 Greene St., manufactured, that differed materially from the French in many points. It was more simple and durable, lighter, stronger, and cheaper. The reach of frame was made of hydraulic tubing, made by gauge, just as sewing machines, Waltham watches, and Springfield muskets were made, so that when any part wore out or was broken it could be replaced at an hour's notice. Its bearings were of composition or gun metal, and the reach or frame was tubular, giving both lightness and strength. The hub of the hind wheel was bushed with metal, and the axle constituted its own oil box. It was different from the

French *veloce* in the arrangements of the tiller, which was brought well back, and was sufficiently high to allow a perfectly upright position in riding. The stirrups or crank pedals were three-sided, with circular flanges at each end; and as they were fitted to turn on the crank pins, the pressure of the foot would always bring one of the three sides into proper position. They were so shaped as to allow of the use of the fore part of the foot, bringing the ankle joint into play, relieving the knee, and rendering propulsion much easier than when the shank of the foot alone was used as in propelling the French vehicle. The connecting apparatus differed from that of the French bicycle in that the saddle bar served only as a seat and a brake, and was not attached to the rear wheel. By a simple pressure forward against the tiller, and a backward pressure against the tail of the saddle, the saddle-spring was compressed, and the brake attached to it brought firmly down upon the wheel.

In 1874 another Parisian, Merchegay, showed that weight would be reduced by using a large front wheel and a small rear wheel, and that the rider should be mounted directly over the axle of the front wheel. These ideas were carried out, and the popular "ordinary" was the result. This machine remained in the ascendancy for fifteen years.

In 1875 touring became popular, and the bicycle showed it had come to stay. The new wheel weighed from 35 to 50 pounds, against 80 to 100 for the old velocipede.

The Popular Ordinary (Scientific American)

The "Rover" (Scientific American, 7/25/96)

There were certain undeniable dangers connected with the use of the high wheel, and accidents were many and serious. At length came signs that the design and construction of the wheel was in a state of transition. There were too many "headers" causing riders considerable injury, so a switch was made to the "Star" bicycle.

In this machine the small wheel was placed in front and the rider was mounted over the axle of the high rear wheel. They were propelled by levers, straps, and ratchets, which enabled the wheel to be geared up, thus introducing one of the most important principles used in the modern bicycle.

In 1877 Rousseau, of Marseilles, introduced the "Kangaroo," in which a smaller front wheel was used. Power was communicated to the axle by means of independent chains and sprockets, to the latter of which power was applied by pedals. This arrangement allowed the wheel to be slightly geared up.

About 1880, Starley introduced his famous "Rover," which really embodied the vital points of the modern bicycle in its form. The wheels were both low, though not of the same size, and the rear wheel was driven by chains and sprockets. The great superiority of this machine over the ordinary was soon recognized. Cycling became more popular, and by degrees the high wheel was abandoned by all the makers.

The pneumatic tire was the greatest of all the advances since Michaux, giving more comfort to the rider than possibly any other improvement.

In 1845 R. W. Thompson patented the first penumatic tire in England, but it was only in 1889 that it was adapted to the bicycle by an Irish veterinary surgeon named Dunlop. The cushion tire, in which there was a hollow space in the rubber, was known as far back as 1870. It became very popular only when the pneumatic tire began to be introduced, and soon gave way to this great advancement.

This boon to bicyclists became a target in the war still going on between pedestrians/equestrians and bicycle riders. Malicious persons threw tacks in the roadway to perforate the pneumatic tires of bicycles, and it was proposed to attach a magnet in front of the forward wheel to pick up the tacks as the machine rolled along.

Since every new stage of development was eagerly used by the cartoonists of the day, of course a caricaturist drew a cartoon with the cyclist represented as carrying such a powerful magnet that it not only picked up tacks, but even drew the nails from the shoes of passersby.

Cartoon—The Magnetic Bicycle (Scientific American, *10/5/95*)

Street Car with Hooks for Bicycles (Scientific American, *11/30/95*)

But bike riders were here to stay, and demanded equal rights with other wayfarers. By 1895 New York City had grown to a metropolis with stone-paved streets and car tracks that made bicycling difficult. Hundreds of wheelers clamored for a way to transport their machines to the open country roads.

In Butte, Montana, the streetcars were provided with exterior hooks on which cyclers could hang their wheels, and the idea appealed to New Yorkers willing to pay for the added convenience.

In Brooklyn, New York, on Sundays and holidays the elevated steam railways became so liberalized that they admitted wheelers and their wheels to the smoking cars, a charge of two extra fares being made for the wheel. Hundreds of cyclers availed themselves of the privilege.

The pursuit of speed through the use of wheels has continued through the years.

2

Early Wheels

IN 1869 THE MONOD IMPROVED VELOCIPEDE emerged, and was hailed as an almost-perfect machine. It was very strong, light, easily operated and controlled. The footrests, or stirrups, were so weighted and hung to the cranks that they were always presented to the surface of the foot. In mounting, or after removing the foot temporarily, no time was lost in pedaling. The brake was always ready for use, since it was operated by the hands through the medium of the steering bar. To effect this, the bar rotated in sockets, and had connected with it a strong line or gut, secured at the other end to the brake lever. By simply turning or rolling the steering bar the line was wound around it, and the steering post was within easy reach of the hands, enabling the rider to keep his arms in a natural and easy position and his body erect. In addition, the saddle, or seat was movable from front to rear or vice versa, so that one velocipede could be adapted to the size of the rider without shifting the crank pins, the saddle being held in place by a simple thumbscrew.

In the prevailing velocipede mania, even doctors entered the lists to add to the controversy. They objected to the machines on the grounds that the labor demanded by the lower limbs tended to produce hernia, or rupture. To combat this, inventors produced vehicles operated solely by the hands.

One was patented in February 1869, by Isaac Samuels of Marysville, Kansas; it was impelled wholly by the hands and arms, the feet and legs merely guiding the machine. The front or driving wheel was about 4 feet in diameter, with which the inventor said he could make 25 miles per hour on a

The Monod Improved Velocipede (Scientific American, *1/9/69*)

21

Samuels's Patent Hand-Crank Velocipede (Scientific American, 3/27/69)

three-wheeler, then changing it to a bicycle as his skill progressed.

The rear axle was crooked, but when the wheels were spread, it was a tricycle, easily managed by anyone. A lever was at the rear, and when the rider had gotten sufficiently sure of himself, he could, by a single movement, reverse the position of the axle by a half-revolution and run the wheels together. These wheels then were one, and presto—the trike was a bike! The wheels were constructed to run on any portion of the crooked axle, so there was no difficulty in holding them at any intermediate point desired, while they were prevented from coming together by a fixed collar, or flange, on the axle at the point where the two angles met.

Tricycles were great for everything but turning corners, but since beginners demanded them, this, too, was corrected. John Tremper of Wilmington, Delaware, designed one simple enough to be built cheaply, safe enough for beginners, swift enough to suit the daring, and convenient enough to meet the demands of short and tall, obese and lean, young and old. It was a three-wheeled affair, the front

level. This wheel was held in the forks of an arched reach, the rear end of which was pivoted to an arched axle. The ends of these formed journals for the two guiding wheels that were about two feet in diameter. The rider sat on a saddle connected to the reach by an upright sliding bar, and was sustained by a spiral spring to give ease of motion. Directly in front of the rider was an upright, through the crosspiece of which ran a shaft, having on each end hand cranks from which rods ran to corresponding cranks on the driving-wheel shaft. These cranks were placed at right angles so the machine could be put in motion from a state of rest, in whatever position the cranks were in. Stirrups were attached to cords that ran to the rear axle and served to guide the machine. When the vehicle was run straight forward a spring fixed to the center bolt of the rear axle held the axle in the proper position. This yielded when pressure was brought to bear on the stirrups, but when the pressure on either stirrup was released, the spring brought the axle to its normal transverse position.

Another objection against the bicycle was the difficult beginners experienced in managing it and balancing on it at the same time. Topliff & Ely of Elyria, Ohio, patented an ingenious device that could be used either as a tricycle or a bicycle, so the beginner had the opportunity of learning on a

The Topliff and Ely Adjustable Velocipede (Scientific American, 3/13/69)

Tremper's Three-Wheeled Velocipede (Scientific American, 3/6/69)

wheel being the driver, as usual, but placed so closely to the axle of the hind wheels as to give as complete command over the motions of the machine in turning corners as the two-wheeled velocipede. From the axle of the hind wheels rose a bow-shaped brace, to which was bolted one end of the reach. This was two parallel pieces of wood, bolted together and embracing between them an upright standard, or pipe, terminating in a forked brace in which the driving wheels turned, and having directly over the wheel's rim, where the fork braces united, a brakeshoe, or pad. The weight of the driving wheel and part of that of the rider were sustained by a spiral spring, which served as a buffer in passing over obstacles. The steering bar—a prolongation of the forked brace—passed up through the hollow standard and was furnished with handles on the top. The seat was sustained by two cast-steel springs secured to the front of the reach by means of a cross strap, or block, and bolt, so it was easily adjusted further front or rear. The upright tube could be adjusted to the reach to suit the length of legs or arms of the rider.

The daredevils were still around, however, demanding more speed, no matter the cost in bodily injury. In March 1869, Richard C. Hemmings of New Haven, Connecticut, startled the world with a unicycle, or the "Flying Yankee Velocipede," as he termed it.

Queer and odd as the appearance of the wheel was, Mr. Hemmings said his thirteen-year-old son propelled the five-foot-diameter wheel at a pace that kept up with good roadsters and did not allow them to pass him.

The main wheel had a double rim, or two concentric rims, the inner face of the inner one having a projecting lip to keep the friction rollers and the friction driver in place, each of these being correspondingly grooved on their peripheries. The frame on which the rider sat sustained these friction wheels in double parallel arms, on the front one of which was mounted a double pulley, with belts passing to small pulleys on the axis of the driving wheel. This double wheel was driven by cranks turned by the hands. The friction of the lower wheel on the surface of the inner rim of the main wheel was the immediate means of propulsion. A small binding wheel between the rider's legs served to keep the bands or belts tight. The steering was effected either by inclining the body to one side or the other, or by the foot impinging on the ground, the stirrups being hung low for this purpose. By throwing the weight on these stirrups the binding wheel could be brought more powerfully down on the belts. Over the rider's head was an

Hemmings's Unicycle or Flying Yankee Velocipede (Scientific American, 3/6/69)

awning, and there was also a shield in front of his body to keep the clothes from being soiled by mud and wet. When going forward, the driving wheel was kept slightly forward of the center of gravity by the position of the rider. By this means the power exerted was comparatively small. The vehicle seemed to be a good way to elude attacking dogs, which were one of the obstacles to cycling then as now.

To return to cycles made for safety more than for speed, C. E. McDonald of Amsterdam, New York, showed an extremely novel model that showed promise. It had simplicity of construction, was cheap to manufacture, and was adjustable. The frame was a hollow pipe, the rear being a complete circle in which the steering wheel rotated on its axis, the driving wheel running between the parallel bars of the front portion. The axle of this wheel passed through boxes secured to the parallel bars by set screws, so it could be adjusted forward or back to suit the physique of the rider. The axle of the steering wheel ran in boxes secured to sliding bars curved to fit the inner diameter of the circular portion of the frame, thus allowing this wheel with its axle to perform an entire revolution within the

frame on a horizontal plane. Its movements were controlled by means of rods attached at one end to the ends of the axle, and at the other brought together to the lower end of a lever directly under the rider's seat, the handle of which came up in front of the rider, the fulcrum being on a cross piece between the rear portion of the parallel bars which served not only that purpose, but also was a brace. The vehicle could be guided by one hand. The seat could be lowered or raised. The reach, which in an ordinary bicycle extended in an upward curve from the level of the rear axle to the top of the driving wheel, was easily made, while in others its forging added greatly to the cost of the vehicle. The adjustable bicycle made mounting much easier, and, if overturned, the machine could not fall upon the rider, as the circular formation of the rear portion forbade a complete inversion. The danger of overturning this machine was further diminished by the weight of the rider being brought nearer the center of suspension, as the seat could be brought very near the horizontal line of the axles without preventing or interfering with the action of the legs.

The "ordinary" hadn't entirely vanished by 1869. It was still being improved, as L. H. Soule of Mt. Morris, New York, claimed when trying to patent his "simultaneous-movement" velocipede. It was, in effect, a unicycle, the small wheel being only one point of suspension for the reach, and acted only as

McDonald's Adjustable Bicycle (Scientific American, 4/24/69)

Soule's Simultaneous-Movement Velocipede (Scientific American, 4/3/69)

a truck or friction wheel. The driving wheel, which was also the steering wheel, could be of very great diameter, as it worked not by direct connection of the feet with the treadles, but by the hands and feet both, through the medium of connecting rods between the cranks and a walking beam. The reach supporting the seat was hinged to the lower end of an upright pivot secured in a yoke at the top of the forked brace, the lower end of which were boxes for the reception of the ends of the driving-wheel axle. This arrangement allowed the wheel to be guided to the right or left, and also to be projected under the seat of the rider, or further in front. By this arrangement, when great speed was desired and the state of the road permitted, the rider could bring the wheel directly under him. In descending grades he could project it in front to guard against the danger of being thrown over. In order to secure the wheel in either of these, or any intermediate position, a sector, notched on its upper side, and forming a portion of the reach, passed through a slot in the yoke, and a spring catch fit into the notches to hold the wheel and reach in the relation desired.

The inventor claimed as advantages over the ordinary two-wheeled vehicle that it was easier to balance when in motion, could be propelled at a higher rate of speed with the same amount of exertion, and could be driven over any ordinary road passable for other vehicles.

Not all velocipedes were made to enhance either speed or safety, as witness a unique vehicle made by John J. White of Philadelphia. It was a utility machine, the wheels of which revolved around a common axis, with crank motions for both hands and feet. The rider sat astride a saddlebar in the center of a hexagonal frame from which uprights rose, connected at the top by an adjustable neck yoke. This yoke could be elevated or depressed to suit the stature of the rider. It was fixed in place by means of spring bolts or catches. The uprights were strengthened by curved braces extending laterally to the axles on either side, which passed through them. They were attached below to the extremities of the hexagonal frame. To these lateral braces the brakes were attached, so they could be put on by lowering the elbows, and were provided with springs to take them off the friction wheels on the axles when they were not required. Two rock bars attached to the inner side of the uprights were connected by short pitmans to the cranks, through

White's Improved Bicycle (Scientific American, 5/29/69)

which the power of the hands was applied. The cranks also received the power of the feet through stirruped rods. Each wheel was independent of the other so the machine could be readily guided or turned about in a circle of twice its width.

For men of ordinary size, the wheels were about 7 feet in diameter, steel-rimmed, with a thick, vulcanized rubber band for the tread. The rims were attached by double wire spokes to flanged central disks fixed to the axles. These wires could be interlaced, if thought best, but in either case the wheel was extremely light and elastic. The wires were stretched by means of nuts inside the flanges of the disks.

The perimeters of the wheels were made light and stiffened by corrugation. The wheels could be strengthened against lateral strain on rough roads by extending the axles and passing additional wires from the periphery to their extremities.

The hexagonal frame that supported the rider was also adjustable on the uprights and lateral braces. The saddle bar could be cushioned or provided with a spring saddle if wanted. Removing the hexagonal frame from the uprights and lateral braces, and removing the yoke, divided the machine into parts convenient for storage and shipment. When set up and in use, it was stiffened by iron rods or braces connecting the uprights with the corners of the frame.

The saddle bar was swung loosely behind so as to be easily thrown off to the right or left. The levers worked by the hands were for guiding, and to counteract the irregularity of the movements given by the feet. Every revolution of the wheel carried the rider twenty-two feet, so the speed was great on level and descending surfaces. Because of the wheel's large curve and elasticity, the machine gave a comparatively smooth ride over any roughness. Also, it was easy for the rider to dismount and pull the machine over obstacles when necessary.

By 1879 the bicycle was firmly entrenched in the American way of life, and races against time and between cyclists were common. The *Scientific American* proclaimed, "The bicycle furor which pervaded this country and Europe a few years ago has subsided into a solid interest in this means of locomotion, which is much more noticeable in England than in this country, although the bicycle is very popular here, and is daily becoming more so. It has arrived at great perfection, and is constructed more scientifically than formally. It is of great practical utility as well as a rational means of amusement. It is, in fact, an ever-saddled horse that eats nothing and requires no care."

The *Scientific American* hailed the "Columbia" as the most perfect bicycle made. It was manufactured by the Pope Mfg. Co., of Boston, Massachusetts, and maintained its popularity for some time.

The machine had a steering head of one solid forging. The backbones, made of steel, were large, light, strong, and rigid. The spring was attached by a joint to a small plate sliding on the backbone. The wheels were of the spider pattern, with V-shaped steel fellies, with forged steel hubs, hardened in bearing parts. The back wheel and pedals ran on coned bearings, one being adjustable, and were made so as to prevent the admission of dust and dirt. The front-wheel bearings were conical and well hardened, and fitted with coned fastenings of India rubber, 1-inch on the front and ¾-inch diameter on the back wheel.

The seat was placed almost directly over the center of the front wheel, by which means a much

The Columbia Bicycle (Scientific American, 1/18/79)

larger wheel could be ridden, thus gaining in speed and making the act of propelling it more like walking, instead of pushing with the feet as in the velocipede.

Long-distance records were being made, and were duly hailed in the newspapers. On November 27, 1877, Mr. A. D. Chandler rode from Leominster to Boston, a distance of 40 miles, in 4 hours. In May 1878 Russell Sharp and John Storer went from Boston to Newport, 72 miles, in 13 hours, including stoppages. Actual riding time was 10½ hours. In August 1878 H. E. Parkhurst rode from Clinton to Boston, 44 miles, in 5½ hours without a stop, making the distance from South Framingham to Boston, 20½ miles, in 2 hours. He also rode from Boston to Natick and returned, without a dismount, 36 miles in 3½ hours. On October 15, 1878, E. W. Pope and F. S. Jaquith rode in the suburbs of Boston, 77 miles in 11 hours, including stops. After having ridden 60 miles they made the distance from Wellesley to Newton, over 7 miles, in 38 minutes. On October 19, 1878, G. R. Agassiz, on the Chestnut Hill road, traveled one mile in 3 minutes 21½ seconds, winning the Boston Bicycle Club Gold Medal. E. Costen and F. Smythe, on September 2, 1876, on a turnpike road, made 205 miles in 22 hours.

Because of the many accidents to which bicycle riders were subjected, at intervals various "safety" machines would surface. In 1883 the Leicester Safety Tricycle was put on the market. On this the rider was placed upon a saddle vertically above the pedals, and could therefore employ the effectual downward thrust so approved by the medical profession. He had before him a safety bar on which he could rest his hands, from which he could steer and apply the brakes, and which also served to prevent his falling forward when moving downhill. The tricycle was a front steerer, which added still more to its safety in the descent of hills. The gearing had the advantages of backward and forward double driving combined in one central endless chain passing from the pedal crank to the axle. Steering was effected by the front wheel, which, from the construction of the entire machine, always had a large percentage of the rider's weight pressing upon it to insure its efficacy. Behind the rider, to prevent all possibility of a fall backward, was a bar or tail, which added also to safety in mounting and dismounting. The brakes acted upon the tires of the driving wheels by a movement of the wrists, the right or left being applied as desired, or both together, while the steering could be done at the same time, and without moving either hand from the safety bar.

The "Coolie" Tricycle (Scientific American, 4/4/83)

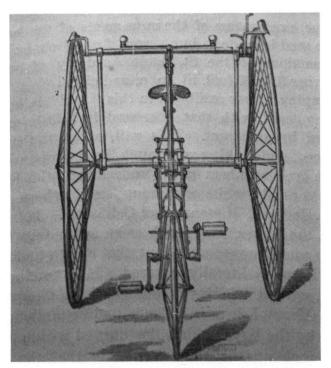

The "Leicester Safety" Tricycle (Scientific American, 4/4/83)

About the same time a tricycle was introduced for use in India and other countries where native labor was abundant, and the climate such that whites found all outdoor exercise impossible. The machine was propelled by coolie power working behind the rider. The brake was applied to a drum on the gearing box. The standard size of the driving wheels was 48 inches, and these could be geared either level or slightly down. For hilly countries, the latter was recommended. It was made single to seat one rider, driven by one coolie, or in double form to seat two riders, propelled by two coolies. The native driver sat behind, pedaling and steering the machine, which became a cheap kind of carriage, requiring no horses, and no stabling or coach house.

Contrary to many beliefs, our ancestors were often "swingers," so naturally an inventor came up with a "Swing Bicycle." Nathaniel Brown of Emporia, Kansas, built the unusual-looking vehicle. Its large wheels were secured to the outer ends of two hollow axles or shafts, which were mounted upon a central shaft, and were formed with ratchet wheels and friction disks. The seat was suspended by means of arms connected to centrally slotted straps passing over the axles. The ratchet wheels passed through the slots in the straps, and were engaged by spring pawls secured to the forward upper ends of the arms. In connection with each of the two

Brown's Swing Bicycle (Scientific American, 2/5/87)

other ratchet wheels was arranged a block, held to the hollow shaft by straps, and provided with a spring pawl engaging with the teeth of the ratchet. Pivoted in recesses in the lower ends of the blocks were lever arms, formed with inwardly extending fingers, arranged so that when the arms were swung toward each other upon their pivots, the fingers were brought to bear against the faces of the friction disks.

The pulling of the levers downward started the main wheels forward, and at the same time swung the seat forward, thus moving the pawls carried by the arms supporting the seat backward, and bringing them into engagement with teeth upon their ratchets, not so far advanced as were the teeth with which they were primarily engaged. As the levers moved forward, the swing of the seat toward its normal position acted to advance the bicycle, and by so reciprocating the levers a pendulum motion was given to the seat. When once started, it propelled the machine for some time.

When it was necessary to turn the machine, say to the left, extra force was exerted on the right-hand lever, which tended to drive the right-hand wheel forward faster than the other. Or the motion of the left-hand wheel could be checked by moving the left-hand lever so that its finger would bear against the friction disk. To stop the machine, both brakes were applied by moving the levers toward

each other. The rider could stop at any desired point, when ascending a grade, and rest at ease, since any tendency of the machine to run backward would be counteracted by the weight of the seat.

By 1887 it was generally admitted that cycle riding was one of the most healthful and delightful outdoor exercises. Even doctors were willing to admit that the movement of the lower limbs in driving the pedals, the gentle force given by the arms in steering, and the constant undulations of the body with the motions of the vehicle, resulted in a rapid and general strengthening of the system. The mere act of riding in the fresh, open air, amid constant changes of scenery, brought on a peculiar cheerfulness and exhilaration of spirits that compensated a thousandfold for all the bodily exertion involved.

Those who had been deterred from the pleasures of cycle riding by fear of accident on the high wheel could dismiss their fears if they used the "Rudge Bicyclette," which had recently been introduced. It was safe in every respect, a header being impossible, the seat of the rider so low he could feel as secure as when on his feet. In fact, his feet were only a few inches from the ground, so even if he fell, no injury would come to him. The wheels were of equal size, the hind wheel being the driver by means of an endless chain, communicating from the hub to the pedals, which were situated between the two wheels. The front wheel was the steerer, so the power required to propel the machine didn't affect the steering as it did in the ordinary bicycle. Because of this, and the closeness of the rider to the ground, a learner could make himself master of the

The Rudge Bicyclette (Scientific American, 6/25/87)

art of riding in a much shorter time, and with considerably less danger than on the ordinary bicycle.

As a runner on level ground, its speed equaled that of other bicycles, and as a hill climber, it excelled. Among other advantages claimed for this vehicle were perfect immunity from headers, very great brake power, easy mounting and dismounting, great power uphill, ease of working against head winds, little vibration and bumping, ability to ride where ordinary 'cycle or tricycle could not venture, no skidding when driving uphill, maximum speed with minimum exertion, comfortable footrests, little splashing from mud and wet, saddle and handles raised at will.

The Rudge gave the form of bicycles to come, and more or less squelched many of the outlandish shapes and devices offered to the public, but the inventors of the day still had to reckon with the most novel of all bicycles still to be offered.

In 1896 Fred Dodson, a boy of fourteen, living at Fishing Creek, Pennsylvania, offered a bicycle for the princely sum of twenty-five cents. It was ingenious and strongly made, and quite good, considering the low price. The vehicle was built of strips of wood and of boards, was fitted with brake and tool box, and it had an adjustable leather saddle having a stretching or tension screw to take up the sag of the leather. It was sold without driving gear, but could be fitted with sprocket wheels and cranks, and with a perforated leather belt in place of a chain. Thus equipped, it was ridable, although not

exactly equal in comfort, easy running, and speed to the modern wheel. The inventor would furnish all this, of course, but only with an increase in price. He could in all truth, however, offer the only wheel on the market whose tire surface was nondestructible.

In 1891 a construction by means of which a bicycle gear could be quickly changed, so that the vehicle could be driven rapidly where the road was easy, or less speed with more power where the road was loose or hilly, was devised. The patent was issued to Frank R. Bigelow, of Gloucester City, New Jersey. Figure 1 shows the device in section applied to the treadle shaft of a bicycle, the bearing of the shaft being supported by an arm in the usual manner. Mounted loosely on opposite ends of the shaft were different-sized sprocket wheels, each having on its inner side a series of sockets adapted to receive the teeth of a sleeve sliding on the shaft, the sleeve being the length of the hub. Near the center of the sleeve was a slot through which extended a pin secured to the shaft, causing the sleeve to turn with the shaft. The sleeve had a series of recesses at each end, forming projecting teeth, as shown in Figure 2, the teeth being adapted to fit the sockets on the inner side of each sprocket wheel, so that by sliding the sleeve one

A Twenty-Five-Cent Bicycle (Scientific American, 2/1/96)

Bigelow's Bicycle (Scientific American, 6/27/91)

29

way or the other, either one of the sprocket wheels could be engaged and driven by the shaft. A hollow thumbscrew was mounted loosely on the shaft and extended through one of the sprocket wheels into the end of the sleeve, which was counterbored to receive it. The inner end of the screw was threaded to engage a threaded portion of the sleeve, and the outer end of the screw had a handle disk, by turning which the sleeve was moved to engage one of the sprocket wheels. In connecting this gear with a bicycle wheel, the latter was provided with two sprocket wheels, one on each side, and preferably of different sizes, the larger one connecting with the smaller sprocket wheel on the treadle shaft and the smaller one on the main wheel connecting with the larger of the treadle sprockets. By then shifting the sleeve, which served as a clutch, either the larger or smaller of the treadle sprockets was engaged, according as the road was easy or difficult.

In the same year a velocipede operated by hand levers was developed by Clarence P. Hoyt, the use of which was calculated to expand the chest and develop the muscles of the arms, while it was designed to be a very strong, durable, and easily managed machine. The main frame consisted of two

Hoyt's Velocipede (Scientific American, *2/21/91*)

vertical bars, while its other end carried a caster wheel. The backwardly extending bars of the frame had bearings for a crankshaft on which was keyed a sprocket wheel, a chain from which engaged a small sprocket wheel on the main axle. Just outside the vertical bars of the main frame, two vertical lever bars were fulcrumed on the axle, a handle piece being secured to the connected upper ends of the lever bars, while a rod extended rearwardly from their lower ends to a pivoted lever bar, from which a connecting rod extended to wrist pins on arms of the crank shaft, whereby, on reciprocating the levers by means of the handle piece, the crank shaft was turned and motion was communicated to the main axle to propel the machine. Extending forward from the caster-wheel bracket, on each side, was a rod passing through a slotted arm secured to the underside of a pivoted pedal, the rods carrying stops in advance of the slotted arms, and the forward ends of the rods being connected to the forward ends of the pedals by spiral springs. With this arrangement, the depressing of a pedal drew upon one of the rods and turned the caster wheel, pressure on the right-hand pedal guiding the vehicle to the right, while the depressing of the left-hand pedal turned the vehicle to the left.

By the turn of the century the bicycle had reached a design much like that of today, but still further improvements were offered. At the New York Cycle Show in Madison Square Garden in 1901, the offerings included bicycles equipped with cushion seat posts as well as spring-suspension saddles. These were attempts at reducing unpleasant vibrations, as was a new "freak" model exhibited.

The inventor claimed much less vibration to the arms through the lever extensions of the handlebar. Their main purpose, however, was to afford a means of propelling with the hands as well as the feet in ascending hills, the upward pull usually exerted on the handlebar being applied directly in helping to rotate the pedals. The machine was steered by the thumbs, which operated the two small loops on the handles of the levers. These loops connected to the steering head through a short handlebar, and moved the front fork without moving the cross bar to which the levers were attached.

In operating this machine the rider exercised his arms as well as his feet. He was obliged to sit erect and bring all the muscles of the body into play, for

A *Foot-and-Hand-Propelled Bicycle* (Scientific American, *1/26/01*)

each of the rear forks of the bicycle. Mounted on one of these shafts alongside one of the pinions was a larger open-gear wheel which enmeshed into the small driving-pinion gear wheel on one end of the rear bicycle wheel ball-bearing shaft, the latter being supported upon the rear bicycle framework. At the upper end of the rear fork was a saddle which was turned in a vertical position when the bicycle was in operation, but could be used in a horizontal sitting position when coasting. There were the usual braking appliances operated from the front handle.

To operate the bicycle the rider, steadying it by the handles, gave it a slight push forward, then jumped upon the two belts, pushing the feet alternately backward down the inclined belt as in the act of walking, raising one foot forward over one belt as the other foot was going backward on the other. The slow movement of the belt was converted into a rapid motion at the driving pinion through the medium of the large gear wheel on the shaft of the rear belt pinion.

The inventor claimed as advantages over the ordinary type the fact that the rider stood erect and brought into action many more muscles than in a sitting position, which was much more healthful and invigorating, while the weight of the body in traversing down the inclined belt assisted in the power of propulsion.

not only did the toes pedal, but even the thumbs were trained to steer. The pull by the arms in climbing a hill was applied direct in a rotative effort, but it was applied under the disadvantage of having the arms bent at the elbow at a constantly changing angle, instead of being straight, as in ordinary hill climbing. This was good exercise for the arms, but it failed to develop the maximum power.

As with most of the unusual innovations, this one made a brief splash, then was forgotten as more exciting developments occurred.

History has a way of repeating itself, even in the matter of bicycles. In 1902 Henry C. Weeks of Bayside, New York, patented a bicycle that was propelled by a person in a walking attitude instead of sitting. The usual sprocket wheel and driving pedals were absent, and in place of them were two spur wheels mounted on each end of a horizontal ball-bearing-supported shaft, one on each side of the bicycle frame.

Means were provided for elevating this shaft to elevate the incline of the driving belts, and the latter were tightened by adjusting the telescopic brace connected with the rear fork backward or forward and securing it with a small nut on the under side. Over these wheels passed two open-meshed broad sprocket-chain endless driving belts which connected with smaller pinion sprocket or gear wheels keyed on two smaller ball-bearing-supported shafts located at the lower extremity of

Weeks's Walking Bicycle (Scientific American, *4/24/02*)

31

3

Make Way for the Ladies

FROM THE BEGINNING OF "VELOCIPEDE MANIA," the ladies clamored to be included in the action. The bicycle was introduced into gymnasiums for ladies, who could exercise wearing the dress commonly used by them in calisthenics. The ones who managed to ride "the beast" were ecstatic, and they caused a rush as their sisters hurried to join in the fun.

Gentlemen were excluded while the ladies practiced, but a few managed to look behind the scenes and observe their better halves performing on their fiery, untamed steeds. The consensus was that they made a very pretty and graceful appearance. There was no reason the ladies should not adopt a special dress for the sport and enjoy it in the open air instead of in a stuffy room.

H. P. Butler of Cambridge, Massachusetts, came forward with a two-seated bicycle with the ladies in mind. The back seat could be used as either a sidesaddle for ladies or an ordinary saddle for men, with both riders assisting in the propulsion. The inventor also had in view the placing of two sidesaddles over the rear wheel to accommodate two ladies, who could then assist in propelling the machine.

Ladies protested the awkward position they were forced to assume astride the iron wheel, and many suggestions were brought forward. One was a velocipede for two persons with seats like a sidesaddle facing in opposite directions to be propelled by the combined power of two riders, each on her own side of the wheel. Another was that ladies don proper attire and use the velocipede as it was. It was argued that the exercise would be much more thorough and helpful than it could be on any such mongrel machine as the one suggested above. It was certain that the ladies could not be left out, so manufacturers began considering them in their plans.

By February 1869, a riding school for ladies had been started in New York on Fifth Avenue at the Somerville Art Gallery. It had two fine halls, each with an area of over 3,000 square feet. One hall was set aside for beginners, the other for those more advanced. An ad stated, "With a proper teacher of their own sex, and with suitable dresses for the preliminary practice, ladies can obtain such a command over the velocipede in one week's practice, of an hour daily, that they can ride side-saddle-wise with the utmost ease."

At Pearsall Brothers' riding school in New York, a three-wheeled machine was placed on exhibition especially for the ladies. It consisted of an easy basketwork seat placed over two wheels. A small wheel projected in front that was guided by a rod passing back to the hand of the lady occupying the

Tandem Velocipede of 1869 (Scientific American, 4/10/69)

Sturdy and Young's Circular Velocipede (Scientific American, 6/12/69)

seat. The rear wheels had a pedal attachment, by which the lady could work up to a moderate speed with little exertion.

Madcaps arose who were not so modest. In Davenport, Iowa, Miss Katie Putnam astonished the citizens by her skillful management of the bicyclical velocipede. To add to the effect, she wore a bicycle garment so startling the newspapers refrained from describing it.

The Messrs. Pearsall introduced their pupils to more difficult performances, one compelling them to mount an inclined plane. A miniature hill was thrown up at one side of the riding room, about 5 feet high, rising at an angle of nearly 45 degrees. Many of the pupils succeeded in passing over it safely, but the majority reached the bottom sadly tangled with their velocipedes. But you can't keep a good woman down for long.

The ladies attended races in velocipede halls where both slow and fast contests were held. In a slow race the rider who took the longest time to circle the hall a specified number of times won, and in a fast race just the opposite held. An outcry was raised when congregations of "roughs" and rude

boys interrupted the action, and proprietors of the halls were advised to exclude such characters by proper regulations.

Once the ladies adopted the velocipede, it provided amusement in many forms. Sturdy & Young of Providence designed a machine to use in private and public pleasure grounds, or to be let by the hour at large affairs and other public gatherings that proved it was possible to provide pleasure at the same time a profit was shown. It combined all the advantages of the circular railway, so popular at Saratoga Springs and other pleasure resorts, with only a small fraction of the cost of such railways. The way was made of scantlings or planks so arranged as to form a circular course upon which the combined efforts of a party of riders could get up an extraordinary speed. The handles were merely for the purpose of steadying the riders, as the apparatus needed no guidance. Each wheel was a driving wheel, and brakes could be attached if desired. The velocipede merry-go-round provided endless amusement for young and old alike, as well as moderate exercise, and many a lady too timid to solo took her first exhilarating ride in a circle where her machine could not topple with her.

Quite a few early tricycles were designed with the ladies in mind. They were safer, and the ladies could settle their full skirts in them much more gracefully than trying to straddle a two-wheeler. Around 1878 Singer & Co., of Coventry, England, produced one that had several valuable features. In the arrangement of wheels, the driving wheel was central with the weight, and the two forward car-

Improved Tricycle (Scientific American, 3/30/78)

rying wheels were equally spaced on either side of the rider. Where a side driving wheel was used, the weight could not be deployed with advantage, and the other side carrying wheel acted as a drag upon the tricycle.

The frame, light but strong, was formed by a fork in front, carrying the pivots and forks for the two forward wheels. After uniting, it arched over the main driving wheel, where it carried the fork for that wheel, which fork was also attached to the main fore carriage fork. The seat could be either a saddle or a cushioned seat, shifted at will by unscrewing bolts and nuts in the end of the bent spring. The other end of the bent spring was attached to a vertical spindle passing through a socket in the forward forging. The height of the spindle could be adjusted by a set screw, so the seat could be fixed to suit the rider's convenience for the freest and most comfortable play to the legs. The driving gear was controlled by two treadles on the end of two levers, which were made into bell cranks by an arm at right angles to the treadle arms. These bell cranks gave an effective pull upon the cranks of the main driving wheel. A splash board was fixed to the main rib passing round the main driving wheel to protect the rider. The steering gear was a powerful and effective arrangement on the two forward wheels. The spindles were carried up through the sockets and fitted with handles at the upper ends. The forks of the two leading wheels had arms riveted to them, and these were connected by a rod

to make the wheels turn together and could be moved by either handle. A powerful foot brake was added to press upon the tire of the back wheel. The machine was safe, easily steered, adjustable to any size rider, and had a brake powerful enough to stop it at will.

Another version also came from England in the same year from Hillman & Herbert. The framework was a horizontal bar, bent into a rectangle, with a double-throw crank axle running in antifriction roller bearings, which were bolted to the frame. Two large wheels, 50 inches in diameter, were mounted upon this axle, one of them being the driver. Three C-springs were bolted to the frames to support the seat. Two rods extending downward carried a steel bar whereon the pedal levers were pivoted. A stout tube connection for the guiding wheel was also bolted to the framework, and was curved so as to be out of the way of the feet and legs, and rendered the machine suitable for ladies as well as gentlemen. The guiding wheel was 22 inches in diameter and ran upon an adjustable double-coned pin in an upright fork, about 4 feet in advance of the crank axle, and exactly midway between the large wheels. Its handle was conveniently pivoted so it could be turned over or reversed, and used to draw the machine when necessary, as in the case of steep hills.

The wheels were tired with Para rubber, and their fellies were of U-shaped steel, while a pow-

The Premier Tricycle (Scientific American, 5/11/78)

erful roller brake was attached to the driving wheel, the lever at the right hand of the rider.

The steel bar carrying the propelling levers was placed as near the ground as safety permitted. It was strengthened by a couple of steel rods projecting under the pedal levers in such a way that the double purpose was served of imparting perfect rigidity to the bar, and supplying a guard or stop in case of the pedal levers and crank becoming broken or unhinged. Without such a guard, serious accidents might occur by the pedal dropping and catching the ground while the machine was in progress. The pedals were rubber-cushioned, and the connections were adjustable to suit length of leg. A step was fixed on the right side for mounting and dismounting, while the back of the seat was arranged to carry luggage.

In the event of an objection to the use of legs to propel, A. C. Johnson of Martin, Ohio, presented a model with four wheels, with only the arms used to move it forward. The rear axle was fixed in the hubs of the rear wheels, and turned in roller bearings on the frame. The driving mechanism consisted of a train of three spur wheels, one being fixed to the middle of the rear axle, another turning in bearings on a triangular frame supported by the main frame of the vehicle, the third and uppermost wheel in the series being mounted on a shaft having at opposite ends hand cranks for driving. The bearings of this shaft were in a movable frame, pivoted on arms projecting from the top of the triangular frame. This arrangement was to allow one or another of three driving wheels on the upper or driving shaft into gear with the intermediate wheel to secure the advantage of more or less leverage over the resistance to be overcome.

Johnson's Improved Velocipede (Scientific American, *3/11/82)*

35

The forward end of the velocipede rested upon a fifth wheel on the front axle, and the latter was connected by levers with a steering foot lever conveniently near the rider's seat. This seat was mounted on springs attached to the rear of the main frame.

The use of four wheels gave a wide base, and the forward or leading wheels ran in the regular wheel tracks of a road, giving, in this respect, a great advantage over the three-wheeled velocipede. There was also considerable advantage in running the machine by hand instead of foot, especially if the upper portion of the body of the rider needed development by exercise.

Children were not overlooked in the development of the velocipede. From the start, models were made especially for them, or the adjustable feature included so the machines could be fitted to them. In 1880 Alfred Vick of Mount Carmel, Connecticut, patented an improved velocipede designed for children. It was propelled by the hands, and could be steered by either the feet or the hands. The body of the velocipede was preferably made in the form of a horse, but it could be made in a variety of other shapes, such as that of a carriage body, a chair, etc. The rear portion of the body was supported upon two wheels placed on axles, A, which were entirely independent of each other, and carried at their inner ends spur wheels, B, which were connected by endless chains with spur wheels on two independent shafts, C, journaled in the neck of the horse, and provided with hand cranks by which they could be turned.

The forward portion of the velocipede body was supported by a caster wheel, whose shank, D, was jointed and provided with an arc-shaped slot, having a notch at each end for receiving a transverse bolt passing through the pintle of the caster. When the strap was not in use it could be hooked up out of the way. The arrangement of the working parts can be seen in Figure 2, which is a partial view with the figure of the horse removed.

The invention was hailed as a pleasant change for the youngsters after using the velocipede propelled by the feet, and also because it would help develop the chest and arms of the rider. It was called a "Cyclepede" and delighted many a child whose parents were wealthy enough to purchase one.

Tots too young to propel a velocipede were not overlooked, either, and the modern car seat had its beginning in an invention patented by Messrs.

Vick's Cyclepede (Scientific American, 7/31/80)

Louis Rastetter and Crist Siebold of Fort Wayne, Indiana, in 1891. The seat attachment for bicycles could be readily put on or removed, adapting the vehicle to hold a child in front of the rider in such a manner that it could not fall out and would not unbalance the machine. It could also be adjusted to suit children of different sizes. The child's seat could be placed on any common form of bicycle. It was supported at the back by the spring of the main seat, a cleat passed through the front coil of the spring being secured to the back of the attached seat, from the lower front portion of which braces extended downward and forward, and were bolted to a support secured to the steering fork and the main frame. The foot rests extended in a nearly horizontal position on each side of the fork, and the rear portions of the foot rests were bent upward and clamped to depending hangers, the clamp being adjustable to suit children of different sizes. The handlebar extended around the front of the seat, forming a secure guard to prevent the child from

Rastetter & Siebold's Bicycle Seat (Scientific American, 10/31/91)

McNaughton's Bicycle Attachment (Scientific American, 3/13/97)

falling out. By this method of attaching the seat, the child had a foot on each side of the fork, and had the same swinging motion as the operator, the weight of both coming together upon the saddle, whereby the child was included in the healthfulness of this form of exercise.

All sorts of attachments were devised to protect the ladies from having their clothing soiled, blown about by the wind, or being caught in the chain or wheel. J. G. McNaughton, of Salisbury, New York, devised one in the form of an eagle to prevent mud being thrown by the rear wheel on the rider, and to protect the skirts of the lady from the hazards of cycling. It was mainly a mud guard, with the eagle's head pointing rearward and his wings extended outwardly on each side. It was rigidly mounted on the frame, and the wings were hinged and provided with springs to keep them distended, while allowing them to fold inwardly should the bicycle fall on its side. Just back of the crank axle were bearings in which were hinged legs, preferably made of a continuous U-shaped bar, having at their extremities claws grasping bearing blocks to contact with the ground and hold the bicycle upright when still.

They were also adapted to serve as brakes. Rigidly attached to the middle portion of the bar forming the legs was an elbow connected to a slide rod, and the latter was connected to a hand lever fulcrumed in convenient reach of the rider, whereby the legs could be thrown down to serve as a brake, or as supports when the rider dismounted.

Theron R. Cherry, of Buckhannon, West Virginia, made a shield for the front of the bicycle, patented in 1896. It was a folding screen attached to the front end or head of a lady's bicycle, there being a screen at each side of the head, adapted to be folded up against it or unfolded and extended past the pedals, to protect the feet and ankles from view when mounting or riding, and to prevent the skirts from being blown about the limbs. The folding, fanlike screens were secured by suitable clips or brackets to each side of the head, the rods of which each screen was composed being covered by any suitable fabric and pivoted together at their lower curved ends, while extending down upon the forward arm of each screen there could be, if preferred, a light leather casing into which the screen could be folded and held in compactly folded position by cords or straps. The curvature of the arms caused the screens to extend outwardly a sufficient distance to avoid the pedals and not interfere with their operation by the feet of the rider.

Cherry's Screen for Ladies' Bicycles (Scientific American, 4/25/96)

A New House Bicycle (Scientific American, 2/20/97)

For those too timid to ride a bicycle outdoors, and also to use in therapy for convalescents and the gouty, there was a house bicycle called the "Hygienique." It was composed essentially of a saddle of variable shape and height and of sprockets connected by a chain with a double crank carrying a brake. It permitted anyone, well or convalescent, to pedal at home without any effort and without fatigue if he desired to take a little exercise in bad weather. It also gave motion to joints made still by a recent attack of gout or rheumatism. The return of strength and mobility soon permitted increasing the length of the exercise, and through the motion of the arms and legs, of obtaining a moderate and salutary sweat.

The hands that held the double crank could, in fact, either simply follow the motion of the feet or cause the motion thereof, the legs remaining passive, or else obtain a great muscular output from the latter through a contrary stress. The apparatus was therefore destined to render the greatest services to those who had need of a moderate amount of daily exercise. It was probably the first reducing machine used.

Speed was the most important factor to men, but comfort was more important to the ladies. In 1905 P. W. Bartlett of Richmond, England, announced a bicycle "as comfortable as a rocking chair" and it was a remarkable mechanical ingenuity. The new machine was fitted with an antivibrating easy-chair-like saddle, which afforded wonderful relief to a tired back and which proved a luxury when coasting down long hills. The ladies' machines met with particular favor. They were of exactly the same construction as the machines built for the men. Besides the chairlike saddle, the machine had another improvement. The handlebars were almost directly under the saddle. It was this arrangement

How the Bicycle Is Ridden (Scientific American, 9/05)

End View of the New Bicycle (Scientific American, 9/05)

that enabled the woman to ride the diamond frame with ease. The steering gear was under perfect control and a smaller circle could be described on this machine than on any other.

The bicycle was therapeutic in many ways. The possibility of cycling becoming a pastime in which the sightless could participate appeared impossible, but the Royal Normal College and Academy of Music for the Blind at Upper Norwood, London, dispelled this illusion by 1908. Among the various recreations provided for the blind pupils at this institution none was so popular as cycling. To enable the scholars to indulge in this sport the school acquired various machines of special design. The most popular was the multicycle devised to carry a team of twelve cyclists. The cycle, which was designed and constructed by one of the foremost cycle manufacturing firms of the United Kingdom, was built up of six two-wheeled members, each adapted for two persons, coupled together, there being a connecting bar between each successive pair of wheels to form the complete train. The machine,

which was of substantial build and devised to carry riders of either sex, had a total length of 28 feet.

Each pair of wheels was a complete unit in itself, including differential gearing in the single axle, and seats for two riders, while the front seat had side handles such as was the practice in the old tandem tricycles. The frame was of special design, the front seats being carried on vertical supports, as was also the handlebar pillar connecting with the axle, while the rear seat was supported upon the raised hump of the bar connecting succeeding pairs of wheels together, except in the case of the extreme rear rider, where the seat was also carried on a vertical pillar from the main framing of the machine. The connecting bar itself was swiveled and the machines were coupled up by this moving joint with sliding pins, the connection in front being made with the steering handlebar column of the preceding machine and at the opposite end to the main frame of the axle to the succeeding unit. By this arrangement perfect lateral play was provided such as was required in negotiating curves, while

A Multicycle for the Blind (Scientific American,
11/14/08)

the system also enabled the train to be split up into sections, such as a quadruplet, sextet, octet, or train for ten riders.

Of course, the machine had to be guided and controlled by a sighted person, who in this instance occupied the second seat, which gave command of the first pair of handlebars. The slightest deviation to either side of the front wheels was transmitted through the coupling bar to the second pair of wheels, the driver of which could act in concert, thereby conveying the same intimation to the third unit, and so on to the end. The drive was of the ordinary rotary type geared to 51 and each rider participated in the propelling action. Even the sharpest curves could be rounded with facility and ease. Each handlebar was equipped with a power-ful brake and the machine could be pulled up dead within a short distance when the whole of the braking facilities were simultaneously applied, rendering it perfectly safe.

The pupils did not confine their participation in this recreation to trips around the extensive grounds of the institution, but under the guidance of a competent sighted captain were frequently seen on the high roads of the neighborhood. From time to time long excursions were undertaken into the country, the longest journey being a round trip to Brighton on the south coast, a total distance of 100 miles. The trip was accomplished in 10¾ hours' actual running time, an average speed of 9.75 miles per hour.

4

Feet Wheelies

WITH ALL THE EXCITEMENT ENGENDERED BY wheels, the dandies of the time felt compelled to exhibit their prowess on wheels. Thomas L. Luders devised a method of speed called the "Pedespeed," which was like no other. Hermes, the messenger of the gods in ancient mythology, wore winged sandals, but it was left to American ingenuity to put wheels on feet that probably made faster time than the Greek Hermes by far.

The Pedespeed consisted of a pair of wheels, some 14 or 15 inches in diameter, to which were attached some stout hickory stirruplike appendages, in the bottom of which were foot pieces, shaped like the woods of common skates.

On one side of the stirruplike appendages were firmly fastened metallic plates, each having a short axle or bearing projecting from its center, upon which the wheels above mentioned turned. The stirruplike appendages were made of flat strips of wood about 3 inches wide in the broadest portion, bent so that one side was nearly straight, while the other was made to meet it about midway to form a sort of loop. In the bottom of this loop were placed the foot pieces, provided with toe straps and a clasp for the heel. To the upper end of the stirrups was attached a piece of wood to fit the outer and upper conformation of the calves of the legs.

With these contraptions on their feet, the young

blades of the day could execute inside and outside rolls, figure eights, and all at an incredible rate of speed. It was a dangerous sport, but the ladies were not left out. When Pedespeeds were worn by them, shields covered the tops of the wheels to protect their gowns. The use of these wheels faded after a short time, due mainly to the high casualty rate of the users, but they caused their share of excitement.

A safer type of skate surfaced around 1882 with the invention of the Tricycle Skate. Unlike ice skates, these could be used year round, if you could find a smooth, macadamized road to use them on. A speed of 20 miles an hour could be attained on such a surface, but since these type roads were exceedingly scarce, roller skates didn't seriously challenge the popularity of bicycles, or come into general use until years later when paved roads and sidewalks grew more general.

In 1901 Paul Jassman, of Brooklyn, presented a chain-driven roller skate. It utilized the downward pressure exerted on skates in a very novel way. The vehicle comprised a frame in which front and rear wheels were journaled and on which guide posts were supported for the purpose of receiving a sliding footrest. Springs were coiled around the guide posts and held the footrest in an upper position. A spring-pressed pawl was secured on the

Thomas L. Luders's Pedespeed (Scientific American, *3/19/70*)

rear of the footrest, which pawl, on the downward movement of the footrest, imparted movement to a sprocket chain by which the rear wheel was driven.

A German inventor also designed a foot-cycle of improved construction, in which the springs for raising the foot usually found in such devices was avoided. The support was thus steady and solid, even when the person was at rest. The driving wheel was located under the center of pressure of the wearer's foot, and this enabled the person to move in smaller circles than with the usual construction. The details of this cycle can be readily understood from the illustration. Two spring pawls were secured to an extension from the foot plate, and were adapted when pressed downward to engage projections formed on an endless chain, but to slide by the same when drawn upward. The chain

was thus driven forward positively at every downward stroke of the foot, and its motion was communicated through intermediate gearing to the driving wheel. A brake was situated on the forward end of the device, which could be operated by downward pressure at the toe to frictionally engage the driving wheel.

After the invention of the automobile and motors, gasoline engines were attached to everything that had wheels. In 1906 M. Constantini, a well-known Paris inventor of carburetors and other devices for automobiles, attracted considerable attention when he motorized roller skates. In view of the fact that each skate contained a gasoline motor, carburetor, battery, and spark coil, the whole had to be reduced to a comparatively small size. Use of rubber-tired wheels gave a very smooth-running

Tricycle Skate (Scientific American, *11/4/82*)

From this reservoir a small rubber pipe specially treated to withstand the deteriorating action of gasoline ran down to the skate and connected with each of the carburetors. A second controlling device fastened to the belt enabled the person to adjust the gasoline feed from the tank to each of the motors. The gasoline reservoir was made to hold from one-quarter to half a gallon of fuel. Owing to its small size and flat form, it occupied but little room and was covered by the coat, leaving nothing visible but the tubes and wire running to the skates. Each motor weighed 8.8 pounds and used a quarter gallon every 35 miles. The weight of the skate complete was 13.2 pounds, and speeds of from 3 to 25 miles an hour were attained. To start, the operator turned on the gasoline, relieved the compression by means of a special valve-raising lever, and then skated along the road. As soon as he was under way, he switched on the ignition current, and the motors began to operate. If the novice didn't take care to lean forward at this moment, the

Chain-Driven Roller Skate (Scientific American, *1901*)

movement. On the back of each skate was a small sheet-iron box that contained the battery and the spark coil. From the box a pair of wires protected by rubber tubing passed up to the leather belt which the person wore, and upon the belt was placed the switch by which he was able to make or break the ignition circuit when he wished to start or stop the motor or to regulate its speed. On the back part of the belt was fixed a small gasoline tank in the form of a flat and slightly curved sheet-iron box.

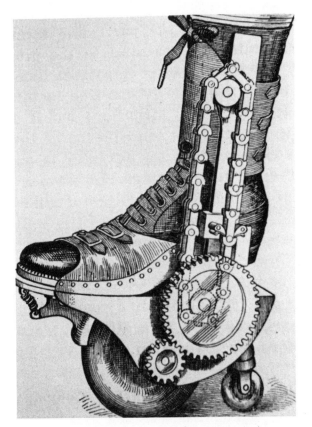

Foot-Cycle (Scientific American)

First Gasoline-Powered Roller Skates (Scientific American, 4/14/06)

sudden acceleration could upset him. To stop, it was only necessary to break the ignition circuit or to raise one's self upon the front wheels. By doing the latter, the driving wheels were raised off the ground and the motors raced, running free. If one motor ran faster or better than the other, the operator could correct this by moving that foot back of the other, or by bearing more weight upon the faster-running skate.

M. Constantini also made another type of motor skate. In the second form the exterior of the skate remained about the same, but otherwise it differed considerably from the first. The main difference lay in the fact that only one of the skates was fitted with a gasoline motor, and the latter was made to drive the second skate by means of a rod which passed across and connected the two. The rod had a universal joint on each end at a point near the skate, and was attached at one end to the motor body and at the other to the frame of the second skate. In this way the rod kept the skates spread at the right distance and made the whole system quite steady, especially as the feet could not spread accidentally too far apart, such as often happened with roller skates. The motor was made larger in this case and had power enough to operate both skates. This form was intended for sportsmen, for races, and in all cases where a high speed was wanted, while the first form was adapted for moderate speeds.

Horizontal Cross-Section of the Latest Form of Motor Roller Skate (Scientific American, 4/14/06)

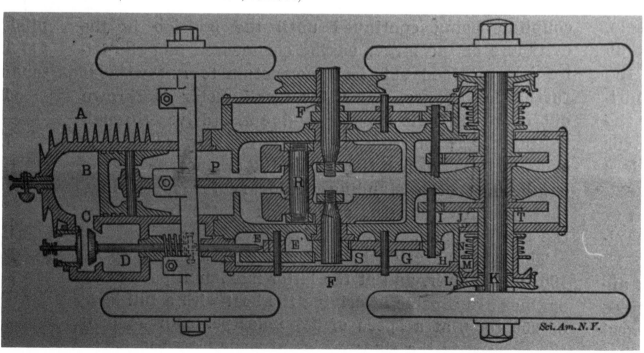

44

In the second form of skate, the available space between the four wheels was almost entirely taken up by the large motor and its carburetor, while the space under the second skate was utilized to stow the gasoline tank, which was of considerable size, and also the battery and spark coil, thus dispensing with the double battery and coil which the first system used. The gasoline tank had a capacity of about a gallon, and this was found upon trial to be enough for a run of 50 or 60 miles. A rubber tube passed across along the rod to take the gasoline over to the motor on the other skate.

A novel feature was the use of two different speeds on the wheels, and this was obtained by the arrangement shown in the illustration. The motor was placed in a nearly horizontal position. The air-cooled cylinder is seen at A, the piston at B, the connecting rod at P, and the crank at R. At C were the valves, which were operated by a rod from the cam, E, the latter being driven by a gear from the motor shaft. This shaft was in two halves, as indicated by the letters FF. From the upper half a set of gears connected with the rear axle. A similar gear train was driven from the lower half. The two gear trains had different ratios and they could be connected with the rear axle by a friction clutch on either side. Thus, on the lower side there was the pinion, S, mounted on the motor shaft, working with the gear, G; and then the pinions, H and I, mounted on a countershaft, and the gear, J, on the rear axle. The latter gear was mounted on a collar, T, which ran loose on the axle. Keyed to the collar and sliding upon it was the friction cone, M, which was pressed down by the spring, N. This cone worked in a second cone, L, which was keyed fast to the axle. By operating a lever, the spring threw in the lower clutch and so obtained a given speed on the rear axle. Throwing out this clutch and operating the upper one gave a second speed from the other train of gears, which had a different speed reduction.

The skates were exhibited at the Paris Automobile Show and aroused so much interest that even the Shah of Persia ordered three pairs of motor skates, and the inventor received several flattering offers for the sale of the English and American patents.

Most roller skates could not be used on ordinary roads because the rollers were of such small diameter that they dropped into every depression and unevenness of the road and checked the progress of

The Construction of the Wheel Skates (Scientific American, *10/26/07*)

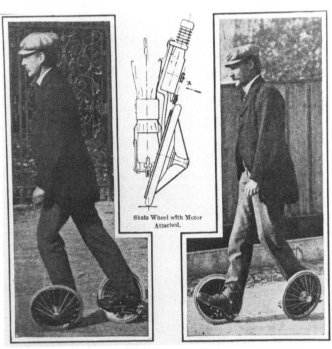

On Level Ground; Brake Lifted

Skate Wheel with Motor Attached

Traveling Downhill; Brake Applied (Scientific American, *10/26/07*)

the skater. What was necessary was a skate with large wheels, but these, if placed directly under the skater's feet, would raise him dangerously high. The difficulty was solved by a Swiss inventor, M. Koller, of Winterthur, in 1907. He designed skates made of a single wheel about a foot in diameter. The skater's foot was supported below the center

45

of the wheel, and in order that the tread would come directly below the center of the skater's foot the wheel was set on a slant. The wheels were dished, comprising a disk of corrugated metal connecting the hub with the rim, and also a series of tension spokes which served to stiffen them. The foot support was suspended on a hanger attached to the wheel axle, and it was provided with a pair of braces extending upward to support a strap which was fastened around the skater's leg above the ankle. To prevent the wheels from rolling backward, a brake was attached to the foot support and bore against the inner periphery of the wheel rim. This brake was normally out of action, but was automatically set as soon as the wheel started to reverse its direction. If desired, this brake could be thrown out of action completely to permit the skater to perform various fancy figures.

In addition to the brake just described, the wheel for the left foot was provided with a rearwardly extending arm which the skater could use as a drag to retard his motion. The wheel for the right foot was provided with a similar drag arm which also had in connection with it a brake block that bore against the inner periphery of the wheel when the drag arm bore against the ground, thus furnishing the skater with a quick-acting brake for use in emergencies.

The inventor also proposed to use a motor in connection with each skate wheel, which would be attached in the manner indicated in the diagram. The wheel would be driven by belts running from the power shaft of the motor to a pulley groove on the felly of the wheel. Fuel for the motor was supplied from a tank strapped to the back of the skater. Although the wheels looked dangerous, it was claimed that the use of them could be learned in a very short time, and that even beginners could acquire the knack of using them with safety in a few minutes.

New skating devices kept showing up, and as late as 1914 Bruce Eytinge presented a pocket-edition motor vehicle using the skate principle. The year before he had offered similar skates powered by electricity, obtaining power from a storage battery carried on the back of the skater, but, not satisfied with their performance, he brought out gasoline-driven skates.

A three-wheel roller skate was employed with 5-inch wheels and a wheel base of 25 inches. The front pair of wheels did the driving, and a belt was

Automobile Skate That Makes 20 to 30 Miles per Hour (Scientific American, 2/21/14)

connected to a twin-cylinder gasoline engine. The base and two crankcases were formed in a single aluminum casting. The driving was done direct from between the opposed cylinders to a pinion between the two front wheels, thus giving a perfect balance. A 3-pound flanged flywheel was carried between the cylinders as best shown in the small inserted engraving. The crankshaft had only two bearings which were located in the adjacent wall of the crank casing. By eliminating the bearings in the outer walls of the casing, the weight was reduced. The motor was of the two-cycle type with 1¾-inch bore and 2-inch stroke, and it developed 1 horsepower at about 1,800 to 2,000 revolutions. A steering post extended upward from the engine and, owing to the dual front wheels, steering was effected by leaning the post to one side or the other.

Attached to the steering post were a gasoline tank and a miniature spark plug, while within the steering post, which was hollow, lubricating oil was carried and fed by gravity to the parts that required it. A battery of four dry cells was carried on the back of the skater, and there was a switch on his belt. The entire weight of the outfit was 30 pounds. With it Mr. Eytinge traveled at speeds of over 20 miles per hour on the streets of New York, and he believed that 25 to 30 miles per hour could easily be attained.

No brake was supplied, but merely cutting off the spark served to retard the skate, owing to the compression in the engine cylinders. By this means the skates could be brought to a stop from a speed of 20 miles an hour in about 75 feet, without using the idle skate as a drag. However, it was much more convenient to make a turn in case an object was suddenly encountered. Very sharp turns could be made because the skater could lean inward as far as he liked to overcome centrifugal force.

A queer little vehicle appeared on the streets of American cities in 1916 that was neither a motorcycle nor motor skates. It was a sort of compromise between the two, and the idea was probably suggested by the "scooters" made by the youngsters from a soap box, a few pieces of board, and a discarded pair of roller skates.

The new means of transportation was known as the "autoped," and was propelled by a single-cylinder gasoline engine. It could attain a speed of 25 miles per hour on a level road. The control mechanism was centered in the handle, which was also used for steering. The autoped was distinctly up-to-date, for it was equipped with a self-starter for the engine. Because of the small diameter of the wheels fitted to the autoped, it was obviously a vehicle for city streets and smooth highways. Its moderate first cost and low operating expenses brought it within the reach of practically everyone.

The great limitations of early ice and roller skates caused outdoor skating to be indulged in for only a few months of the year, and then only for sport. In 1917 Charles H. Clark of New York City invented a

By Means of These Skates One Can Travel Three Times as Far with the Same Amount of Effort. (*Scientific American, 3/17/17*)

The Autoped, a Gasoline-Driven Vehicle Which Is a Compromise Between Motor Skates and Motorcycle (Scientific American, 9/2/16)

new form of skate that he said would be the seven-league boots of people who wanted to travel. In 1904 Mr. Clark had been the Pacific Coast champion wheelman, and he solved many of the problems involved in the use of skates for transportation.

The inventor thoroughly understood the possibilities of this mode of locomotion, devising a skate that could be used almost anywhere and at any time, and using his invention on the streets of the city. The skates, with their ball-bearing, pneumatic-tired wheels, ran easier on a good road or street than ice skates would slide on ice, and they would also climb any hill. There were two 9-inch wheels on each foot, located on opposite sides of the foot. The front wheel was on the inside of the foot and the rear wheel on the outside so they did not interfere with any movement of the legs. A brace on the outside of the leg was journaled to the foot rest, while the upper end was attached to the ankle, relieving the ankle of any strain whatsoever. This brace also acted as a brake arm to set the hand brake on the rear wheel. In earlier models the inventor used a roller tire brake and placed the brace on the side of the leg, but both of these expedients proved unsatisfactory. In the skates shown either brake was operated by simply pushing either foot forward, as a person would naturally do at any time he wished to stop. The tires used for the wheels gave sufficiently to allow the skate to be readily steered, and on the whole the skate oper-

ated very much like an ice skate. However, the feeling was quite different, since the skater glided over a cushion of air and felt no jar. He simply swung from side to side, raising first one foot and then the other from the ground.

The road skate was made in various sizes, and the heaviest man-sized model weighed only 4 pounds each, despite the substantial construction. One great advantage a skate had over any other form of wheeled vehicle was that a person could carry the skates with him to the locality where he wished to skate, thus saving the journey on skates to and from that locality. Furthermore, skates could be taken into any building and carried about without great inconvenience.

As a foot-propelled vehicle, the skate was most efficient because the propelling force was applied directly to the ground, hence no transmission system with its attendant losses was necessary. The skate was noiseless, regardless of the surface skated over, whether rough or smooth. It could be used for business as well as pleasure, and it was even possible to use it extensively for the rapid transportation of soldiers in favorable localities, although in the war zone in France, where the roads were next to impassable, it would be necessary to build either permanent or portable skate courses in the localities where troops were to be moved. However, it is doubtful that any army ever adopted this means of troop movement.

A Near View of the Pneumatic-Tired Road Skates, Which Are Provided with Brakes Operated by the Braces (Scientific American, 3/17/17)

5

Water and Ice

FROM THE TIME THE VELOCIPEDE GREW POPU-
lar, people were determined to put wheels on
every conveyance—or else fix every roadway and
river so they could be used by cyclists. Suggestions
were made to cover the Croton aqueduct with
pavement from the Westchester side of the Harlem
River to Central Park, in New York City, as a grand
"boulevard" or highway for velocipedes, complete
with an ornamental rail on each side and a low
central rail to divide the north and south travel.

Barring these drastic measures, inventors began
to alter boats by adding velocipede parts to propel
them. When the water froze in winter, they
modified their velocipedes to travel on ice.

An early device from a Boston man was quite
neat. A velocipede was mounted in the center of a
boat to propel it through the water. The rudder was
worked by two cords passing from the steering bar,
over pulleys fixed upon the side of the boat below
and in front of the operator, and from thence back
to the tiller.

Harper's Weekly published an engraving of an
ice velocipede. The frame of this velocipede was
built like those commonly used in New York City.
It had but one wheel, steered with a bar as in the
land machine, but armed with sharp points to
prevent its slipping. Instead of the two wheels

behind, there were two sharp steel runners, like
those attached to ice boats. This machine could be
propelled with astonishing rapidity.

M. Jobert exhibited a new river velocipede at the
Maritime Exposition held in 1876 in Paris. It was
composed of two cigar-shaped floats made of tinned
plate, united by a platform of very light wood,
which carried the seat of the operator. The mechanism was also attached to the platform, and it
consisted of a paddle wheel, with two cranks on the
axles, with straps for the feet. The action was
exactly like that of a land velocipede. To steer the
device, a light rudder was placed in the rear of the
apparatus, and it was handled by the cords passing
round a pulley turned by the handle in the hand of
the operator. It was simple, easy, and very speedy.

In 1883 James B. Bray of Waverly, New York,
patented an improved velocipede sleigh. The apparatus was to be ridden and propelled in a manner
similar to that of the velocipede or bicycle. The
backbone was supported by two pairs of runners,
the front pair being swiveled. The propelling wheel
was mounted in a forked frame swiveled in the
backbone or main frame, and provided with spurs
projecting from its periphery. The outer ends of the
crank shaft were connected with the front runners,
so that when the wheel was turned for steering, the

Water Velocipede (Scientific American, *4/3/69*)

New Water Velocipede (Scientific American, *1/ 20/77*)

Ice Velocipede (Scientific American, *3/6/69*)

Bray's Velocipede Sleigh (Scientific American, *9/1/83*)

front runners would turn in the same direction. It was guaranteed to secure a high speed on snow or ice.

At the same time, H. S. Blanchard of Cairo, Illinois, patented an ingenious vehicle for traveling by land or water. The inventor chose the form of a swan as being the most graceful and appropriate for the purpose. A light framework of wood or iron was covered with sheet metal, waterproof canvas, or other material. From the body of the vessel arose a standard supporting an awning, which, by means of adjustable guys and a ball and socket joint, could be fixed at any angle to be used either as a shelter from the sun or storm, or as a sail.

But the principal means of propulsion were paddles and rotating floats worked by the feet of the rider, who sat on a seat forming a part of the steering lever or helm. From near the top of the standard, curved arms projected outside the vessel, having suspended and supported on the water ellipsoidal floats that steaded the vessel on the water and aided in supporting it on the land. As a protection from injury the floats could be surrounded with wire netting. These floats, as well as the vessel itself, were filled with cases of cork or other buoyant material to insure floating even if the outer case was injured.

Propulsion was secured by the action of hinged floats connected with a platform treadle which carried cone floats, to the rear ends of which the operating paddles were hinged. As the platform

Terry's Boat Tricycle (Scientific American, 2/16/84)

Blanchard's Quadricycle (Scientific American, 6/16/83)

was rocked in one direction the cones were advanced forward, the paddles floating horizontally. By the reverse motion the paddles turned against the broad ends of the cones and presented their surfaces to the water. A double crank shaft could also be connected with the foot platform and treadle so as to rotate floats at either side of the vessel as another means of propulsion.

If the vessel was to be moved on land, the buoys served as supports and as wheels; or the outer ones could be removed and those connected with the crank shaft be used as a means of propulsion, the buoy in front being used as a guide wheel.

A year later, in 1884, a man in England showed a novel tricycle capable of being converted into a boat. When used on terra firma, the apparatus was like an ordinary two-wheeled velocipede with steering wheel behind. The operation of converting it into a boat was very simple, and took but half an hour. The two large wheels were made in two parts and fastened together by bolts. Two sections, placed parallel with each other at a distance of a meter, were used to form a space for the rower to occupy. The other two sections, fixed vertically, and external to the first, served to give length and to make a boat with rounded ends. Two steel tubes, which connected the small wheel with the body of the tricycle, served to fix the two parallel sections at

The Same Converted into a Boat (Scientific American, *2/16/84*)

their upper parts and to hold them at a distance. A wooden rod which was of no use in locomotion on land, was passed beneath and in the center of the sections, keeping them in place and answering as a keel. The frame of the boat was completed by a cord, which, starting from the extremity of the upper part of one of the vertical sections, connected the extremities of all the rest with each other, and served as a support for a tarred canvas that covered the whole boat with the exception of the central space reserved for the oarsman.

All mounted, the apparatus formed a decked canoe combining all the conditions necessary for proper buoyancy, even at sea. The buoyancy was increased by two air bags of 20 liters capacity each, which were attached to the two sides at the upper part of the open space.

The inventor, a Mr. Terry, crossed the English Channel safely in his machine, but then was arrested when the customs officers thought they had encountered a new sort of smuggler. However, the matter was soon straightened out, and Mr. Terry folded his boat back into a velocipede and toured France.

Another ice velocipede slid into being in 1885 when Joseph Hussong, of Camden, New Jersey,

presented it for inspection. The frame upon which the runners were mounted consisted of two bars united to a vertical standard at their forward ends, and at their rear ends curved downward so the runners could be secured to them. The shank of the forward runner, the turning of which served to guide the machine, was journaled in the vertical standard, and was operated by a lever within conventional reach of the right hand of the rider. The drive-wheel frame was pivoted upon a cross rod joining the sides of the main frame. The shaft of the wheel was journaled in the rear free ends of this frame. The driving wheel had sharp points on its periphery, and was centrally fixed upon the shaft, which carried a sprocket wheel driven by a chain passing around a larger sprocket wheel on a crank shaft provided with the ordinary form of pedals. By means of the left-hand lever arm, the wheel could be raised clear of the ice or pressed downward with considerable force. When this lever was thrown forward to elevate the wheel, the points of two brakes, one attached to each of the rear ends of the main frame, were lowered so as to scrape along the ice. Both of the brakes and the wheel could be held just clear of the ice, by placing the lever in a notch in a rod projecting forward from the seat bar. A

Hussong's Ice Velocipede (Scientific American, *12/26/85*)

spring was so arranged that it could be made to vary the pressure of the wheel upon the ice.

In 1888 Herman H. Holtkamp of New Knoxville, Ohio, patented a simple and cheap attachment for bicycles or tricycles that enabled them to be used on ice or snowy ground. A runner or shoe was arranged for connection with the small wheel of the vehicle, the shoe being attached by means of a clip on an adjustable bracket, whereby the runner could be used in connection with wheels of different diameters. To the large wheel were secured as many attachments as necessary, each consisting of a cylindrical metallic plate, lined with leather or other slightly yielding material, and having flanges extending outward from the side of the cylindrical section. This section was arranged so it could be passed over the rubber tire and the felly of the large wheel, and on its inside were two projections extending toward the hub of the wheel, adapted to received a clamping bolt, by which the attachment was clamped to the wheel. The two outward bottom flanges of this cylindrical section were placed at either side of the center of the tire, in order to allow for the regular operation of the bicycle brake, the small wheel being lashed to the backbone of the bicycle. With this attachment the vehicle could be freely used on ice, or heavily packed or frozen snow, while the attachment could be connected to or removed from the bicycle in a very short time. The whole combination, made of steel, could be sharpened for special feats on very smooth ice.

It remained for the genius of a citizen of Chicago to devise a machine for both use and pleasure to enable his fellows to travel with great speed either on land or water, switching easily from one to the other. Thor Olson managed this in 1892 by combining tricycle and boat, or boats, so connected that

Holtkamp's Attachment for Bicycles (Scientific American, *11/10/88*)

Olsen's Cycling and Boating Machine (Scientific American, *10/8/92*)

they operated together perfectly on either element, although it took only a moment to separate the boat from the tricycle.

The machine consisted of twin boats rigidly connected and a tricycle attached to the boats so ingeniously arranged that the machine was propelled and steered by the same mechanism. This machine had the most perfect stability in either element, was light, attractive looking, and produced lively interest when exhibited because of its originality. In this device the traveler could carry his necessary baggage, tools, and hunting and fishing tackle, yet the whole device without a load weighed but from 50 to 75 pounds. While it was arranged to carry only one person on land, its buoyancy was such that it could carry three or more persons on the water. Thus the traveler, the pleasure seeker, and the military man would not be hindered from reaching his destination because of floods, washed-out bridges, or no bridges or pontoons.

The English Channel was always a worthy adversary when man attempted to cross, either by swimming or on some new invention deemed

The Pinkert Navigating Tricycle (Scientific American, 9/8/94)

adequate for the feat. In 1894 a man named Pinkert invented an aquatic machine of the tricycle type on which he attempted to cross the awesome channel. The machine consisted of three hollow wheels, airtight, with paddles fixed upon their exteriors. The wheels might have been called magnified rubber tires. The wheels were worked by crank pedals after the manner of the bicycle. Pinkert attempted to cross the English Channel from Cape Grisnex, France, to Folkestone, England, a distance of about twenty-five miles, but difficult for navigation by small craft. On a calm day he rolled down the shore to the water's edge, and then, with the assistance of man to push, he worked out through the breakers and headed for old England. It was pretty slow work, but the inventor bravely continued his exertions. After many hours of labor, when he was halfway across, the tide turned. Pinkert was sure he'd be carried away from land, so he hailed a passing vessel and was taken on board. His first attempt had failed, but he would probably make further experiments.

The next year Evaristo Fernandez of New Orleans patented a bicycle construction designed to travel with equal facility on land and ice, or in the water. The wheels were preferably of copper, their side plates inclosing a large central air space. The rear wheel, forming the drive wheel, had lateral blades on its sides to engage the water when the bicycle was so used, and its felly was toothed to enable it to take hold of ice when the rubber tire, which was only designed for land use, was removed. To hold the bicycle upright when used in the water, side weights were connected by suitable bails to the wheel axles. When the machine was used on land, these weights were raised by chains which passed through a tube depending upon the frame bars, links of the chain engaging a stop or pin to hold the weights raised. The saddle of the machine was of a form designed to prevent the water from splashing up against the rider. It had a lateral mud and water guard at its rear.

The workings of the house, and of less adventuresome souls, were not overlooked. At a cycle show in Paris in 1897 a prominent bicycle manufacturer presented a novelty called "Velo-douche," which was an eminently practical device for combing exercise and the morning ablutions. The device was a combination of the home exerciser and shower bath, and it enabled the rider to obtain any amount of exercise desired, with or without the

A Marine and Land Bicycle (Scientific American, 9/14/95)

A Velocipede Shower Bath (Scientific American, 4/10/97)

bath. The machine consisted of a shallow tub to which was secured a framework carrying a bicycle saddle, a handlebar, pedals, sprocket, wheel and chain. The resemblance to the bicycle went even further. The small sprocket wheel, which was driven from the large sprocket on the main shaft by the medium of a chain, was secured to a small rotary pump fastened at the rear of the frame. The suction piece of the pump ended near the bottom of the tub and the discharge pipe was curved, ending in the sprinkler arrangement common to all shower baths. A cock halfway up the discharge pipe permitted the water being turned on to the sprinkler or through the hose and nozzle, depending on whether or not a bath was desired.

It was, of course, possible to obtain the exercise without getting wet, the pump furnishing the resistance necessary for the exercise and the water pumped being discharged by means of the rubber tube and nozzle. When the rider had exercised sufficiently, he could reach backward and turn the cock so as to let the water pass upward and out of the sprinkler. The harder he pedaled, the larger the stream.

It was possible to direct a stream of water on any part of the body by means of the nozzle connected with the rubber tube. The tub could be divided

into two compartments, one containing hot water and the other cold water, and the cold and hot shower be used at will. The device could be made to set in any ordinary bathtub, and foresaw a use in cycle clubs, riding academies, sanitariums, and the army.

In 1902 an American inventor hit upon the idea of using his bicycle to drive an ordinary catamaran. The bicycle was suitably supported above the two connected boats, the rear wheel engaging two friction rollers. The shaft of one of these friction rollers carried a pinion meshing with a gear carried on the second shaft. By propelling the bicycle in the usual way, the rear wheel, acting through the medium of the friction rollers and the transmission gearing would turn the paddle wheel and drive the catamaran forward.

In the same year, because he wanted to use his vehicle in all kinds of weather, Benjamin C. Trudell of Bay City, Michigan, invented what he called a "winter velocipede," on which runners took the place of wheels. The driving gear consisted of a spur gear fixed to the crankshaft of the bicycle, and a pinion meshing with the spur gear, the shaft of which was rotatably mounted in a bearing carried

Bicycle-Driven Catamaran (Scientific American, 3/1/02)

by the lower end of a bracket secured to the bicycle frame. The opposite end of this shaft carried a gear meshing with a pinion rigidly attached to a spiked driving wheel. By rotating the main spur gear through the medium of the pedals, the spiked wheel was turned forwardly.

In order to adjust the height of this driving wheel and to enable it to yield when overriding obstructions, the inventor resorted to a peculiar device. A vertically movable arm was pivoted to the lower end of the bracket carrying the bearing previously

A Bicycle on Runners (Scientific American, 3/1/02)

referred to. An upwardly extending adjusting rod was fixed at its lower end to this arm and was secured at its upper end to the bicycle frame. A collar secured to the lower part of the rod opposed the thrust of a spring, which resisted the upward thrust, thus permitting the driving-wheel to override obstructions.

In 1906, polar explorer Walter Wellman decided to build a trial motorized towing machine. It took some doing, as every prominent automobile concern had more orders on hand than could be filled, and to undertake an experimental machine such as Wellman wanted "would throw the entire factory out of its stride." After weeks of searching, Charles M. Miller & Bro., of Washington, detailed George W. Wells, an automobile expert and a man of much originality in thought, to build the machine. In a stable in an alleyway in the northeast part of the city, where the desired secrecy could be had, the work was done.

The motor and tri-car frame used were secured from a motor bicycle maker, but everything else was constructed by hand under Wells. The motor was of 4½ horsepower. It was intended for towing solely and not for speed and therefore geared low. The machine could travel from 2 to 30 miles an hour over smooth ice.

The runners used were of two pairs of Norwegian "skis," both having seen actual service in the North on Wellman's former trips. The wood was seasoned and could be relied upon. They were reinforced, however, with sheet iron, underneath which were steel runners or skates. The front "skis" were the guides; the rear ones being used to take some of the weight from the tractive or driving wheel when soft snow was encountered, which was frequent enough in the frozen North to make such a provision necessary.

The driving wheel was Wells's invention. It was constructed entirely of steel except for the rubber tire. The width of the wheel proper was about 6 inches, on the outer edge of which were broad teeth that gave the power in the snow or soft ice. In the center was a pneumatic tire of rubber 2 inches wide. This was covered with steel wire to prevent puncture, and this latter was covered with a strip of leather which was filled with sharp steel teeth about the size of the head of an ordinary screw, which could grip the hardest ice and, as Mr. Wells put it, could climb the side of a house.

There were many water-propelled machines, but in 1909 a young French inventor presented a model

Wellman's Motor Bicycle Sled (Scientific American, 6/16/06)

The Amphibicycle Traveling on Water (Scientific American, 5/1/09)

to be used on either land or water. To enable it to run on water, he attached to it a pair of cylindrical floats, a propeller, and a rudder. On leaving the water, the cylinders and nautical gear were lifted so as to allow the wheels to run on the ground. The cyclist could then pedal his machine in the usual way. Because the cylinders could be made of very thin sheet metal, they didn't add much weight.

The two cylindrical floats, which ended in a conical point, were attached to the bicycle frame by jointed supports so that they could be raised and lowered as desired and could be fastened in place

when the cycle was on the road. For operating the propeller a rubber-covered friction wheel was employed, which was mounted behind the tire of the rear cycle wheel, the small wheel's motion being transmitted by a bevel gearing to the propeller shaft. By using the proper combination of gearing, the propeller could be reversed. A small rudder was mounted at the front, and was controlled by a rod passing from the front cycle fork into the water.

The two cylinders were braced across by a rod which passed between the wheels and also by

The Amphibicycle Traveling on Land (Scientific American, 5/1/09)

The Floats Fold Up for Land Travel (Scientific American, 8/3/12)

A Spin on the Water (Scientific American, 8/3/12)

another, like rod in the rear of the machine. The whole machine weighed about 270 pounds.

By 1912 a Californian owned a contrivance of his own making that would convey him over land at a rate of 20 miles per hour and on water at the rate of 15 miles an hour. He called the device a "hydro-motorcycle." It consisted of a motorcycle equipped with two canoe-shaped metal floats, each 14 feet long and about 16 inches wide. Each canoe was divided into three airtight compartments and was fastened on a light steel-tube frame. When it was desired to make a water craft of the motorcycle, the two floats were simply reversed on their hinges and clamped down by a simple device. The propeller, carried behind the seat when not in use, could be dropped down into the water to propel the craft. The propeller drive contained a clutch which connected the power with a 3-foot propeller shaft of ¾-inch steel. The propeller had three 12-inch blades. Steering was effected by means of two small rudders, one on each of the floats, and both connected to the handlebar of the motorcycle. The total weight of this amphibious vehicle was 425 pounds, of which 225 pounds represented the weight of the attachment.

6

Variety Wheels

MANY AND VARIED WERE THE USES OF THE velocipede by 1883. Because of the smoothness of railroad tracks and their easy grades, they were the target of many velocipede devices.

George S. Sheffield of Three Rivers, Michigan, offered a vehicle that was to prove quite useful to the railroads of the time. It was very light, weighing only about 125 pounds, and was therefore easily removed from the track when occasion required. It had a wide range of application, and was of great utility to railroad men, for roadmasters, engineers, superintendents of bridges, telegraph-line repairmen, track supervisors, wood and tie inspectors, track walkers, and others whose duties took them over the track for various purposes. By using the tracks, no attention need be paid to guiding or balancing the vehicle.

The machine was easily propelled, even at a speed up to 18 miles per hour. The frame, wheels, and arm were readily removed for storage or shipment. Power was applied to the rear wheel by a hand lever in front of the operator and by stirrups for the feet, which were connected with the propelling machinery by levers. The handle between the levers controlled the brake. If required, the machine could be constructed to carry two persons. The tread of the wheels was cast iron, and in the construction of the machine iron and wood were judiciously combined to form a strong yet light and compact vehicle.

Sheffield's Velocipede Hand Car (Scientific American)

59

In 1892 a novel rail-fence bicycle was put in use to transport passengers between Mount Holly and Smithville, New Jersey, by a company that had been organized to construct what was known at the Hotchkiss Bicycle Railway system.

Each passenger furnished his own motive power. A special form of bicycle was required, although the ordinary saddle, handlebar, and propelling mechanism were nothing new. The handle was not required for steering purposes, but was used simply as a means of convenience for the rider when in motion. The frame was double, extending down below the track rail on either side, a distance of 2½ feet, and had at the lower end a small guide wheel running horizontally, which served to keep the machine in upright position, and absolutely prevented any possibility of jumping the track. The front wheel was the driving wheel, and was 20 inches in diameter. Like the other riding wheel, it was grooved to fit the rail.

The track rested upon a foundation of cross ties 3 by 6 inches by 3½ feet, which were placed at intervals of every 6 feet, and upon them rested wooden posts ordinarily 3½ feet high. These were secured to the ties by bolts and angle irons. Narrow wooden stringers connected the posts, and the top stringer had a T-shaped rail fastened to it on which the bicycle ran. Side tracks were placed at suitable intervals, at which the bicycles could be stored when not in use and at which point passengers could be supplied, leaving the machines at any station where they wished to disembark.

What was more than likely the first suspended cable car appeared about 1900. It was called the "Mono-Rail Track Velocipede," a truly novel vehicle of the time. The suspended railway upon which it traveled was suspended by means of hook-shaped plate steel supports from the apex of a couple of inclined poles, the hanger resting on the tops of the poles by means of a pair of plate straps riveted to the hanger and to the saddle. The rail was a continuous built-up I beam, the upper flanges of which formed the track.

The velocipede was suspended from and formed part of a two-wheeled truck, the forward wheel of which carried on its axle the sprocket, which was engaged by the chain drive. The suspended frame was built of bicycle tubing. To enable the machine

The Rail Fence Bicycle Railway (Scientific American, 4/16/92)

The Mono-Rail Track Velocipede (Scientific American, 5/12/00

to be run in either direction, it was provided with two handlebars, one on each vertical member of the frame, the saddle being reversible in the seat post. Each handlebar was provided with a brake lever which, by means of sliding rods attached to the vertical members of the frame, enabled the rider to press a brake shoe against the under flange of the suspended railway.

Lively minds were adapting the velocipede to many uses other than those involving the railroads. England pioneered many innovations, especially on the tricycle, which was used as an object of both utility and pleasure. In 1885 the camera was also undergoing improvements. The slow and complicated processes of dry and wet collodion were replaced by a simpler thing, thanks to gelatinobromide. Excursionists wanted to bring back pictures of the things they'd seen, so Rudge & Co. brought out a photo-tricycle called the "Coventry Rotary." The camera was mounted on a universal joint that allowed it to assume any position and take in the subject to be reproduced in just a few minutes. Three boxes, each containing six plates, 6½ by 4¾ inches, were within reach of the hand, and could be quickly substituted for each other as they were needed. The photographic apparatus could be either left on the tricycle itself or placed on a tripod when the best point of view was not otherwise accessible. It was an innovation highly appreciated by amateurs who cultivated the arts of both tricycling and photography.

Novelties made only for novelty's sake were also spotted at various times. In 1894 reports came in about a hardy individual seen on a curious-looking machine indeed. It was dubbed the "Eiffel Tower Bicycle," and constructed on the same principle as an ordinary safety, except that it had a frame superstructure which carried the rider some ten feet from terra firma. The machine was frequently seen on the avenues of New York City, and the rider easily overtopped the ordinary lamp posts along the route of travel. He had perfect control over the machine, driving it at a good rate of speed and taking sharp corners with perfect ease and apparent safety. The bicycle was mounted from behind in the usual way, but it had to be held by attendants while mounting. The owner sometimes placed the machine against a wall and mounted from a standstill, but in the city this was not always practicable.

The Eiffel Tower Bicycle (Scientific American, *12/1/94*)

Photographic Tricycle (Scientific American, 9/19/85)

61

There was considerable difficulty in driving the bicycle uphill, owing partially to the weight, the length of the sprocket chain, and the balance of the machine. The sprocket chain extended from the upper sprocket wheel to the rear wheel, and the lateral swing or play of the chain was prevented by a guide roller mounted just above the back wheel. The front wheel measured 28 inches, the rear wheel 36 inches, and the extreme height was said to be 13 feet. The machine was constructed in England, but the American Dunlop tire was applied after it arrived in America. The adventurous spirit seen riding this remarkable wheel was usually accompanied by a number of companions who served as a sort of bodyguard and prevented vehicles and pedestrians from obstructing the way.

By 1896 even the police had gotten into the act. The bicycle was introduced into municipal services in New York with excellent results. At first it was experimental, but since Police Commissioner Andrews was a wheelman himself, he pushed for the use of wheels in the ranks. Four policemen were mounted on bicycles and assigned to duty in the upper part of the city. In a short time they were arresting reckless drivers and speeding cyclists.

A New York City Cyclist Policeman (Scientific American, *1/11/96)*

To arrest a driver, the officer rode ahead of the offending vehicle, allowing himself margin enough to dismount and make the arrest. In the case of a cyclist who was obdurate, the officer in one case ran into him, bringing wheels, officer, and cyclist down in a heap, but, as the commissioner expressed it, with "their man on top."

Commissioner Andrews told of one man who had recently been promoted to the position of roundsman for meritorious arrests with the aid of a bicycle. Although a foot patrolman, he impressed into his service on each occasion a private wheel, mounted it, and caught his men, who otherwise, on account of their long start, would have escaped.

The next move was to mount roundsmen on wheels. The duty of a roundsman involved the overseeing a large district and the control of the patrolmen who were performing their tours therein, and a bicycle-mounted roundsman was the ideal officer for the work. For patrol work the cyclist policeman could cover his round four or five times where the foot policeman could do so but once. In the case of an equestrian or mounted policeman the difference would probably be as great, as the horse was kept at a walk not exceeding a pedestrian in speed.

The invention of accessories was keeping pace with improvements in machines. One that was extremely necessary was an improved night light for riders. One of the first electric lamps surfaced in 1896. It was a small magneto-electric machine, operated by a friction and band wheel furnishing current for a miniature incandescent lamp. The little magneto had a shuttle armature, the core of which was thoroughly laminated. No commutator was used, but the current was collected from the frame of the machine, one terminal being grounded, and from one of the bearings which surrounded a slip ring on the shaft. Thus the construction was of the simplest. The alternating current was carried to a low-voltage, two-candlepower lamp, which was enclosed in a reflector of an ingenious pattern. It was a double parabola and concentrated the light at the focus of the outer parabola, from which it was thrown forward in a remarkably powerful beam, which could furnish illumination for quite a distance ahead. The slightest rotation of the bicycle wheel caused the lamp to glow. The lamp had a short, stumpy filament, and was therefore not liable to break from any cause except excessive current. The friction

An Electric Bicycle Lamp (Scientific American, 2/1/96)

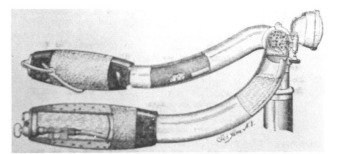

Handlebar Used as an Acetylene Generator (Scientific American)

The mechanism, which was quite simple, was mounted on an iron frame made to fit into that of the machine. On this frame were stretched piano wires, while on the crosspiece were some small hammers operated by pins on the cylinder, and made to strike the wires. The cylinder was rotated by worm gears placed at its left-hand end and driven from the crank shaft by a cord and pulley.

The inventor foresaw the time when the rider would tire of the music by providing a small lever for throwing out the gears and thus stopping the cylinder. The tune could be varied by putting in new cylinders, and the time of any air could be quickened by increasing the speed of the wheel.

An ingenious device for keeping cool on a bicycle

wheel could be disconnected from the tire when light was not wanted, and the transmission had a dust shield.

In 1901 two inventors from Chicago presented another light, a bicycle handlebar gas generator, saying that the hollow bicycle handlebar would be ideal as a carbide and water compartment for an acetylene bicycle lamp. In carrying out this idea, the handlebar was divided into two chambers, the one constituting a water receptable and the other a gas-generating chamber, containing the carbide packed in a porous bag. Between the water and carbide compartment was a gas chamber having an outlet with which the lamp was connected. The water and carbide chambers were connected by a conducting pipe, the passage of water from the water chamber to the carbide chamber being controlled by a valve operated from one of the handles.

Aesthetic delights were not overlooked by inventors, either. At the turn of the century one Samuel Goss of Chicago designed a bicycle that furnished music for the rider of the wheel and his companions to break the monotony and give entertainment during long and tedious runs.

A Musical Bicycle (Scientific American, 8/4/00)

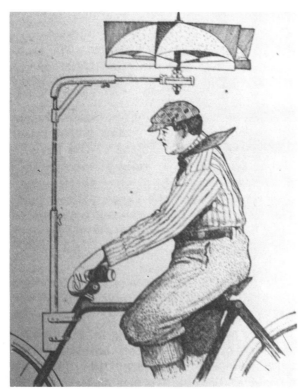

A Bicycle Umbrella-Fan (Scientific American, *11/8/02*)

The Ferguson Cyclograph (Scientific American, *5/28/04*)

was offered in 1902. A combined fan and canopy was invented especially for the use of riders. The canopy was made in the form of an ordinary umbrella, and was provided with a number of blades. As the cyclist spun along, the wind struck the blades and rotated the umbrellalike canopy. Thus the rider was both cooled and protected from the sun. The canopy was carried by a frame which could be attached to the bicycle as shown in the illustration. When not in use, the frame could be readily taken apart.

In 1904 an apparatus called the "cyclograph" was devised by a Mr. Ferguson, and was for the same purpose as the pedograph he invented earlier for automatically making a topographical record of the ground traversed during a journey. The new apparatus differed from its predecessor in that it was designed for the bicyclist, while the pedograph was designed for the pedestrian. It consisted essentially of the flat box arranged horizontally upon the handlebar of the bicycle and containing a sheet of drawing paper, which, owing to the meridians that are traced upon it, may be kept constantly in position in the direction of the road according to the indications of a compass mounted upon the top of the

box. As a result of the motion of the bicycle, the paper always moves backward in the direction of the longitudinal axis of the bicycle, and a small inked wheel rubbing over the paper inscribes a line upon it. If the bicyclist makes an angle upon the ground, he turns the paper (guiding himself by the indications of the compass) at an equal angle in the opposite direction. This was always done around a point situated beneath the marking wheel as a center. The paper immediately continued its motion backward as before. As a result there was marked upon the paper a line which exactly indicated the trip made. The motive power for actuating the cyclograph was obtained from a very simple eccentric arrangement fixed to the front wheel. A disk of thin steel, with an interior eccentric circle, was placed in the vicinity of the spokes of the wheel in such a way that it could revolve freely with the wheel without striking the fork. Upon the periphery of this disk slid a shoe forming part of a lever which was secured, in such a way that it could oscillate, to a small bracket projecting forward from the axis of the wheel outside of the fork. When the apparatus was not in operation, the lever could be dropped out of contact with the disk. The apparatus could be easily started again by raising the lever until the shoe touched the edge of the disk.

The compass was constructed so as to assure its needle a magnetic moment as great as possible, and a moment of inertia as small as possible. Two steel needles were fixed to a small piece of wood through

The Cyclograph on a Bicycle (Scientific American, 5/28/04)

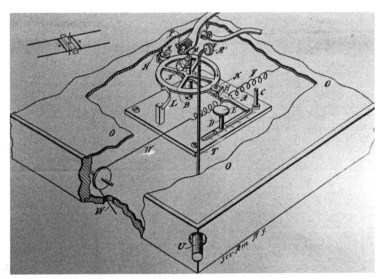

Details of the Mechanism of the Cyclograph (Scientific American, 5/28/04)

which passed the vertical axis. Two small springs served to regulate the equilibrium. The two points of the axis moved in agate bearings. The bottom and cover of the compass were of glass to permit the rider to see through it the meridians previously inscribed upon the paper and to keep them parallel with the needle. The compass was placed about 10 inches above the box in order to protect it against the magnetic effects of the rolling machine.

In order to avoid vibrations, the compass was mounted upon a rectangular frame of strong copper wire fixed by a hinge to the cover of the box, upon which it could be turned down. The compass was capable of revolving upon this frame, and it was held by two independent rods parallel to the surface of the box. The vibrations were thus subdivided and absorbed by eight movable and elastic parts.

In the experiments that were made with the apparatus, the results were such that it was scarcely

possible to distinguish the lines thus obtained from those found on an official map. Even before the apparatus was put on the market, a sample was ordered by the intelligence branch of the English government with a view to utilizing it in China, the topography of which country had been but slightly studied, although the country was provided with good roads. The Ferguson cyclograph was expected to be of great value.

Since flat tires were no stranger to any cyclist, an automatic bicycle pump was invented by P. J. McGuinn of Salisbury P.O., Rhodesia, South Africa. It was an ingenious device designed to be attached to the bicycle wheel and operated automatically to inflate the pneumatic tire of the wheel as the wheel rotated. The controlling levers which set the pumps in action were conveniently located on the upper cross bar of the bicycle frame, so that the rider could readily set in action either the pump on the front wheel or that on the rear wheel, or both, as desired. The pumps were not of ordinary form, but were curved so as to parallel the rims of the wheels, to the spokes of which they were attached. Flexible tubes connected the pumps with the inflating nipples of the tires. The curved piston rod of each pump was provided at its outer end with a crosshead to which a lever was attached. This lever was fulcrumed to the hub of the wheel, and at its opposite end carried a pin which engaged a slot in the head of a short trip lever. The latter was pivoted on a clip attached to the spokes of the wheel. Each pump was operated

An Automatic Bicycle Pump (Scientific American, *1/18/05*)

by an arm pivoted to the forks of its respective wheel. This arm was positioned in the path of the crosshead on the piston rod, so that as the wheel rotated, the piston was forced into the pump cylinder. Fastened to the spokes just above the pump cylinder was an inclined metal plate which, when the piston had been forced home, engaged the operating arm and lifted it clear of the crosshead. As the wheel continued to revolve, the operating arm engaged the trip lever, drawing the piston out again. This action continued as long as the operating arm was in the path of the lever and crosshead. Normally, the operating arm was lifted, against the action of a spring, by the controlling lever, to which it was connected by means of a wire.

Although it was devised for a bicycle, it was obvious that it could be used on an automobile or any other vehicle equipped with pneumatic tires.

By 1910 it seemed as though the bicycle was incapable of further improvement, but inventors kept trying. An Austrian perfected a unique crankless bicycle, for which a large saving of power was claimed. Two long levers and a chain ran over several pulleys. The rider consequently did not move his feet in a circle, but only up and down, which was far less tiring than the old way. For this reason, and the peculiar design of the levers, a saving of 50 percent in human power or gain of 50 percent in speed was secured. The feet rested on pedals fitted at the end of a pair of long arms. A single chain connected the two arms, running first up over two pulleys, and then to the rear over two sprocket wheels fastened to the hub. The chain halves then went forward and were united on a

pulley fixed to the inclined frame tube. In the hub there was a free wheel ratchet device whereby first one and then the other sprocket served to drive the hub. One portion of the chain was always tight and rotating one sprocket wheel, while the other was loose. The rider could alter the degree of transmission at will from high speed to low speed during riding. He could press down the levers an inch or a whole foot, or as far as the length of chain permitted. He could also lengthen or shorten the swinging arms to vary the leverage.

Crankless Bicycle With Sprocket Gear (Scientific American, *11/12/10*)

Chain Gear of Crankless Bicycle (Scientific American, *11/12/10*)

tion when traveling slowly around a steeply banked curve, the roller was made adjustable under control of a small hand wheel, whereby it could be thrown in or out so that the rider could adjust himself as nearly as he desired to the perpendicular. The roller frame could be detached at a moment's notice and secured to the bicycle and the supplementary forks raised, permitting the wheel to be ridden over an ordinary road.

A Track Inspector's Bicycle Fitted for Road Travel (Scientific American, 9/2/11)

Devices already in use were always subject to improvement, especially when it concerned the railroads. In order to lighten the work of the plodding track-walker a French inventor designed an attachment for a bicycle which would permit the machine to travel on the rails, thereby allowing the man who inspected the track and roadbed to cover a larger territory in a given time and with much less fatigue.

The attachment consisted of supplementary forks secured to the main forks of the front wheel and provided at their lower extremities with rollers adapted to bear on opposite sides of the rail. In addition to this there was a light steel frame secured to the main bicycle at the rear which carried at its outer end a small roller that rode on the opposite rail of the track. This served to keep the two wheels of the bicycle on the rail without any effort or steering on the part of the rider. In order to permit the rider to preserve a comfortable posi-

In Use on a Railroad Track (Scientific American, 9/2/11)

7

A Biker's Heavenly Highway

A FANTASTIC CONSTRUCTION IN SOUTHERN CALIfornia known as the "Pasadena Cycleway" was completed at the turn of the century and opened to the public for bicycles and motorcycles. Southern California had special attractions for the wheelman as the season was year-round. Winters were really the most delightful time. The country took on a coat of green and was radiant with wildflowers. This and the assurance of good roads all over the state brought numbers of riders, a conservative estimate placing the wheels in Los Angeles and Pasadena, resident and visiting, at 30,000, and the inventors of wheels at 5,000.

The Pasadena and Los Angeles cycleway was a movement to provide the wheelman with a perfect road, with a minimum grade between two cities nine miles apart and at different altitudes. The inventor and promoter of the novel scheme was a wealthy resident and trustee of the city of Pasadena, Horace Dobbins, president of the company; the vice-president was former governor H. H. Markham. The cycleway, believed to be the only one of its kind in the world, was an elevated, perfectly adjusted road running from the heart of Pasadena to the plaza of Los Angeles. In appearance it somewhat resembled the elevated road in New York, being as high in places, but it was built of wood instead of iron,

yet strong enough to bear the equipment and car service of an electric road. The photo shows the section leading from the depot in Pasadena proper to the site of the former Raymond Hotel. Here it made a turn and continued on to South Pasadena, then through a beautiful country flanked by green hills, with everywhere a view of the range of the Sierras, which were often covered with snow. One object of the cycleway was to give a scenic route through one of the charming localities of southern California.

The portion shown was but half the roadway, for when the cycleway was completed, it was twice as wide, which permitted another innovation, the automobile, to run upon it, making a sky route to Los Angeles for these vehicles.

The cycleway was a remarkable piece of engineering. The proposition had been to give wheelmen a grade from Los Angeles to Pasadena uphill that would not be appreciable, and this was accomplished. The roadway ranged from 3 to 50 feet in height, giving a maximum grade of but 3 percent, and this but for 2,000. At all other points it was not greater than 1¼ percent. This was about the grade of Broadway in Los Angeles in the heart of the city, and not noticeable to the average cycler. The cycleway, with its heavy wire sides painted dark green, was not an objectional feature as it

Bird's-Eye View of the Cycleway (Scientific American, 7/14/00)

the region. They were very abrupt, and surrounded an attractive little valley, and were in reality the broken-up foothills of the Sierra Madre range.

Here the cycleway had its casino at the crown of one of the most beautiful of hills, Merlemount, as it was called, stood in the center of a park of 100 acres, reached from the cycleway by walks, wheel, or motorcycles on beautifully laid-out paths. The casino was 200 feet long, surrounded by a broad piazza and protected by a wealth of tropical and semitropical plants. At one end was a circular rack for ladies' wheels and a ladies' waiting room fitted up in the Turkish fashion. Besides these there were reception rooms, cafe and restaurant, while part of the basement was a Swiss dairy complete in all its furnishings.

From this hill one of the most comprehensive views in southern California was seen. The Sierra Madres—a wall 6,000 feet in height—overshadowed the San Gabriel Valley, not 10 miles distant. To the east rose the peaks of Mount San Antonio, Mount San Jacinto, and Mount San Bernardino (sentinels of the land of the orange and olive), rising 9,000 and 11,000 feet in the air on the edge of the great California Desert. To the south and west, the blue waters of the Pacific glistened in the sun, and twenty miles out to sea could be seen the island of Santa Catalina. The intervening coun-

wound its way through the hills like a gigantic snake. The first half was wide enough to hold four wheels abreast. The timber used in the construction was Oregon pine—1¼ million feet of it—and 20 miles of heavy wire netting.

At intervals of 200 feet over the center, incandescent lights were placed, which at night converted the cycleway into a gleaming serpent. The terminal stations were Moorish in design, one placed near the Hotel Green in the business section of Pasadena, and the other at the plaza in Los Angeles. At these buildings, which were equipped with the facilities of a railway depot, there was also a department for renting bicycles and motorcyles, and a repair shop.

The route of the road was selected by the inventor with great care, and as a result of several years' work in securing rights of way and legislative action. The track ran through Pasadena, South Pasadena, Highland Park, down the picturesque Arroyo Seco, following the Los Angeles hills into the city. These hills formed a picturesque feature of

"Glenarm Curve" on the Cycleway Between Pasadena and Los Angeles, California (Scientific American, 7/14/00)

try was the garden spot of the state, with acres of lime, lemon, orange, and olive trees and almost all the important fruits of the world.

In the picture is the "Glenarm Curve" on the cycleway between Pasadena and Los Angeles.

The cost of the cycle—$187,500—was insignificant when everything was considered. The toll was ten cents by book tickets between Pasadena and Los Angeles (18 miles), the park and other features were free. This toll permitted a bicycle or motorcycle to enter the cycleway and ride up and down all day, if desired. It was estimated that if half the wheelmen in the two cities patronized the road once a month, it would give the cycleway an income of $20,000 per year. This was a conservative estimate as the roads on Sunday between Los Angeles and Pasadena were often filled with wheelmen, who rode through the dust, taking the heavy grade between the cities without question. That the majority of them would choose the perfectly smooth road was without doubt. If the cycleway was successful, it was thought there would be others all over the country, especially in the vicinity of the large cities.

8

That's Entertainment!

ANOTHER ROADWAY IN USE AROUND 1903 WAS not quite so safe as the Pasadena Cycleway. A. M. Schreyer built an inclined structure, a fraction of a curve, and a platform a few feet long—that was all, and it was noble in its simplicity. The chute was nearly 100 feet high, and after pedaling the relatively few feet of almost horizontal planking, Mr. Schreyer would detach himself from his wheel and dive 105 feet through the air to a shallow tank. He did this almost daily to the shock and delight of the spectators who'd paid to see him.

The chute was a light wooden structure measuring 98 feet in height at its top and 35 feet high at the lower end, or what might be called the "jumping-off place." The total length of the structure was 215 feet. The floor of the raceway was formed of slats placed three inches apart. A stripe of black paint indicated the center of the path. There was a slight curve at the lower end of the incline and this curve in turn gave way to a nearly horizontal pathway which was slightly tilted. The dive began about 20 feet from the end of this section. The pool of water was 78 feet away and was 38 feet long, 8 feet wide, and 4 feet deep.

It would seem at first sight that, if this feat could be successfully performed, it could be repeated every day with as much precision as riding a loop, but this performance was one in which the conditions were constantly changing and in which psychology played an important part.

Before riding, Mr. Schreyer gave himself half an hour of quiet and then mounted the lower end of the pathway. Here he studied the position of a flag beyond the pool, which was adjusted to meet various conditions of wind. He then mounted to the top, where his helper held his wheel. He carefully observed every feature of the landscape and, when he felt his nerve at its best, released himself and pedaled down the incline at railroad speed. It was not recorded when the last performance took place, but A. M. Schreyer took his place in the list of daredevils trying for speed.

There were many variations of daredevil stunts using bicycles. The Théâtre du Moulin-Rouge of Paris had its "Circle of Death," and the Folies Bergère its "Terrible Ring." Both were what might be called "aerial velodromes." The track of the former was a kind of bottomless saucer or truncated cone, composed of laths, separated by a space of 2 to 2½ inches. The walls were inclined at an angle of about 70 degrees. Through the laths it was possible to see everything that passed within. This aerial

A. M. Schreyer One-third Down the Incline of the Chute (Scientific American, 6/13/03)

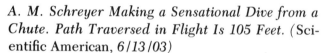

A. M. Schreyer Making a Sensational Dive from a Chute. Path Traversed in Flight Is 105 Feet. (Scientific American, 6/13/03)

The "Circle of Death" (Scientific American, 7/18/03)

velodrome measured about 22 feet in diameter at its middle. The track itself was about 7 feet wide. By means of steel suspending wires, the ends of which were wrapped about windlasses, it was possible to raise and lower the track. The most astonishing evolutions were performed when the track was raised about 16 feet from the stage.

Dan Canary's "Circle of Death," exhibited at Madison Square Garden, New York City, was still more complicated. The bicyclist mounted by a long helical spiral until he reached the circle itself, situated at a height of 60 feet above the ground. In order to emerge from the circle, the bicyclist ascended to the edge of the ring and entered a path which plunged down at a frightful incline.

Perhaps the record for tricks of this kind belonged to Miss Lottie Brandon, who did things in New York compared with which the feats of the men who rode through the "Looping-the-Loop" apparatus and the "Circle of Death" seemed tame. The track was vertical. In order to acquire the necessary momentum, speed was gotten up on a pair of rollers journaled in the lower part of the circle. When a sufficiently high speed was attained, the rollers were dropped by an arrangement of levers, and the bicyclist whirled around the circle, which measured about 16 feet in diameter. To stop the bicycle was a more difficult task than to start it. On the descent, a powerful brake was applied, so that the speed was considerably reduced, in order to enable the performer's manager to snatch her from the wheel as she came dashing down. The wheel itself was carried on by the momentum.

Another invention of an ingenious wheelman of Berlin, Bottner by name, was a double loop that he happily performed the feat of passing through on his wheel. It was the pinnacle of mad daring. The performer, after he had passed through half of the large loop and with his head still down, had to guide the wheel into the smaller loop and out of it again, his head being again turned toward the earth, upon the finishing arc of the larger loop. The velocity with which the performer was hurled through these two loops can only be imagined, but

The Elevated Bottomless Cycle Whirl (Scientific American, 7/18/03)

Looping the Double Loop (Scientific American, 6/25/04)

A Combined Cycle-Whirl and Loop-the-Loop (Scientific American, 7/18/03)

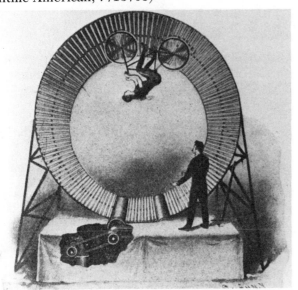

the audience appreciated the stoical quiet of the rider's nerves, his rare skill in managing his wheel, and above all the presence of mind necessary for a successful exit from the whirl.

Since the greatest possible speed was necessary to overcome the resistance offered by the two loops, the starting point was placed somewhat higher than ordinarily, and the first descent quite a little steeper; the retarding stretch was also built steeper than ever before. The whole performance was a ride of death in the true sense of the expression.

Not to be outdone was Proctor's 23rd Street vaudeville theater in New York. They exhibited an indoor racing track on which expert riders daily performed. This track, instead of being made oval in shape, with the ends banked, as was usual in outdoor practice, had to be made circular in order to fit on the stage. It formed an inverted, truncated cone of slats with diameters across the top and bottom of 25½ and 14½ feet respectively. The slats of the cone were set at an angle of 45 degrees with the stage and were 8 feet in length. Within this miniature track several bicyclists performed. Starting at the bottom of the cone slowly and carefully, they

The Cycle Whirl (Scientific American, 3/1/04)

circled around it with increasing speed, climbing higher and higher toward its upper edge while their bodies leaned more and more toward the inside and finally reached a position where rider and wheel seemed nearly horizontal as they went spinning over the clattering slats.

They had a pacer on a stationary trainer who increased the pace, and the pointer of the indicating dial plainly showed the audience the increase as the quarters and halves were run. The racers went faster until they were circling the track in one mad whirl. When a pistol report sounded, the riders plunged to the stage, leaving their wheels, and made a dash for the top of the slats. The one who reached the top first was considered the winner.

A trick rider also soloed on the inclined track, riding around it and plunging from top to bottom and vice versa till it seemed as if he would surely run off the upper edge or be dashed onto the stage at the bottom. He used an electrical bicycle arranged with insulated copper-wire brushes that rubbed on the spokes of the front and rear wheels. Flexible wires from above were connected, one to the brushes and one to the frame of the wheel. As he circled around the track in semidarkness myriads of brilliant sparks were showered from the wheels, producing a very pretty and dazzling effect. Then he rode around the circle with hands off, and repeated the feat with a boy on his shoulders.

In 1909 a performance in Germany attracted much attention. A cyclist traveled outside a globular cage on a narrow wooden path using an ordinary bicycle of 28-inch diameter. The globe was 10 times as great, or 280 inches with a circumference of roughly 880 inches. The globe was rotated by the

These two illustrations represent a remarkable bicycle trick which attracted considerable attention in Germany. (Scientific American, *10/16/09*)

A Globular cage 280 inches in diameter is frictionally rotated at high speed by an ordinary bicycle. (Scientific American, *10/16/09*)

Schreyer on His Stationary Pacing Machine (Scientific American, *3/1/04*)

friction of the cycle wheel on the top. It made 30 revolutions per minute, or 1,800 in an hour, a distance of 25 miles. The cyclist had to be careful to keep in the center of the path. By far the greatest difficulty lay in the fact that his weight constantly drew him down the slope in front as well as backward. In other words, he not only had to keep his balance right and left, but also forward and backward. The latter feat was accomplished by accelerating or retarding his bicycle.

Another act was for two men inside the cage to rotate the globe through the frictional contact of their wheels with the globe.

There were so many daredevils willing to perform and so many variations of loops and sloped tracks that they soon palled. They were fundamentally questionable acrobatic feats and always presented more or less danger to the life of the performer. The novelty wore off and soon the acts disappeared from the programs, particularly since they were too often attended with trifling and even serious accidents.

9

War Wheels

SINCE THERE ALWAYS SEEMED TO BE ONE WAR or another going on, from the time it first grew to popularity the bicycle was considered fair game to adapt to transport troops and messages in an efficient manner. By 1887 armies in Europe included companies of velocipedists. Germans used them for carrying dispatches, as did the French. It was usual, during campaigns, to see smartly uniformed men carrying packs and rifles speeding along with urgent messages tucked in their blouses.

The English had already gone beyond using the velocipede to send messages, developing a multicycle to carry men, guns, and ammunition, and even act as a fighting unit. It was a truly curious apparatus, consisting of a series of six cycles each carrying two men, and hauling a small vehicle loaded with ammunition.

The bicycles were arranged in single file instead of two or four abreast, thus facilitating the operation of the apparatus and diminishing the surface of resistance to the wind. The speed on a good road varied from 9½ to 15 miles per hour. The rubber tires were made in such a way as to secure them from being injured, even on roads that were somewhat rocky.

The starting of the whole was under control of the man who sat in front. The vehicle could turn easily in a much smaller space than could have been done by an ordinary carriage, and could turn while going at great speed without any accident resulting. The men selected to maneuver this multicycle were all volunteers, expert cyclists, and capable of executing all military maneuvers.

Other units were smaller, but equally efficient. A body of cyclists, ten in number, with officers and bugler, marched in usual order of half-sections—that is, by "twos"—until attacked by cavalry. At the command "Halt! Prepare for cavalry! Form square!" each man dismounted. The second half-section moved up alongside the first half-section so as to form a line of four men in front and rear, with a half down, so as to stand in a reversed position, resting on their handlebars and saddles.

French Military Velocipedists (Scientific American, *11/30/89*)

Use of Velocipedes in the English Army (Scientific American, *11/30/89*)

Drill of English Military Bicyclists (Scientific American, *11/30/89*)

Lastly, each man, as he lay prone or knelt behind his machine, set his wheels spinning round with a touch of his finger. Such a fence, apart from the menace of bayonets behind it, formed an obstacle that few horses would face. The men inside, in perfect security, could pick off the advancing horsemen with deadly effect.

The position, so far as mounted horsemen were concerned, was practically impregnable. The infantry rifles, with which cyclists were armed, had great advantages in accuracy and steadiness of aim over the carbines of dismounted cavalry.

Wherever there were wars, there were casualties, so a bicycle ambulance was invented. It consisted of the chief parts of two bicycles from which the trailing wheels and the treadles had been removed. A bamboo bar was securely strapped to the trailing or curved bar and lay above the bicycle seats—holes being made in the under surface of the bamboo, so as to admit the projecting pins or pivots over each wheel. The bamboo then kept the upper parts of the wheels apart at a suitable distance to admit a hammock, which was attached to the bamboo by its ropes and had its ends resting on the two seats of the bicycles.

The tails of the bicycles were turned inward toward each other, and two light teakwood rods were attached to the jaws of these tails, one on each side, by the bolts or axles of the missing trailer wheels. These bars kept the lower parts of the structure rigidly apart. Two cross bars were strapped to the handles of the bicycles and passed under the longitudinal bamboo. The cross bar over the rear wheel had two light iron rods with hooks attached to it. These hooks fitted into eyes or staples in the bamboo so as to keep the rear wheel in plane with the bamboo, the iron frames, and the teakwood rods. The front wheel with its cross bar was free to turn about a vertical axis, as usual, in order that the ambulance could take curves and be guided.

Four men with a little training could run the ambulance easily and safely. They each held the central bamboo with one hand and grasped the end of a cross bar with the other. They could tilt the wheels to one side when they wanted to admit or let out the invalid from the hammock.

For hospital or field service, plain stretchers or hammocks with stiffened sides could be used, and could be slung over easier springs than those under bicycle seats. But the wheels could only be used over smooth ground, and had to be as small and light as possible so the men could lift the ambulance over obstacles and rough ground, or when they had to turn sharp corners.

Once an idea was presented, improvements resulted as the years passed. Aside from military operations, bicycle ambulances were used for a long time, even after the advent of the automobile under certain circumstances.

In the coal mines of Great Britain there were many mishaps, and a cycle ambulance was the vehicle that could reach an injured man despite the rough nature of the road and the cramped headway. The Lancaster coal-mining district had a Rescue Training School in 1908 where miners from each

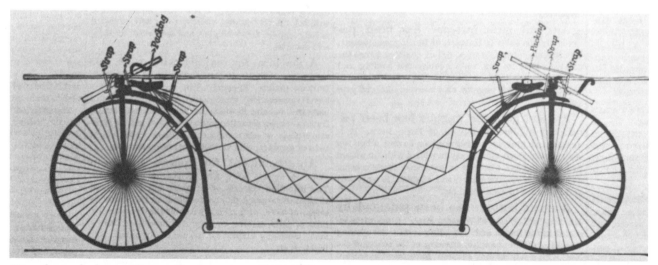

Bicycle Ambulance (Scientific American, 7/30/87)

Simonis Ambulance Bicycle, Which Can Be Converted into an Ambulance in Three Minutes (Scientific American, *10/17/08*)

The Cycle Ambulance Ready for Use (Scientific American, *10/17/08*)

right-hand rail, but it kept its equilibrium by a metallic arm terminating on the other rail in a small wheel. It was a crude apparatus whose two heavy main wheels were connected by a compact body, the various parts roughly shaped, and weighing no less than 110 pounds.

Primitive as it was, it exhibited some very original peculiarities. It was actuated by both the arms and the legs of the rider, but since the rider didn't

mine were instructed in the use of various rescue apparatus for succoring their comrades after a colliery disaster, and the cycle ambulance was a most important piece of equipment.

In war or peace, the bicycle was a most versatile vehicle. In 1894, when Russia was in a state of turmoil, a bicycle was devised to inspect railroad tracks for possible bombs or obstacles put on them to wreck trains, especially before a train carrying the Czar passed over them.

In reality, the word *bicycle* was a misnomer for this police service because the vehicle rested upon three wheels. Its two principal wheels rested on the

Bicycle for the Inspection of Railway Tracks (Scientific American, *5/12/94*)

have to occupy himself with steering, he could devote his entire attention to its propulsion. Two levers, actuated by the arms, connected with each of the cranks of the bicycle at their lower extremities. The Russian railway bicycle employed the ordinary gait of a man's trot—that is, it caused the rider to put forward at the same time the right arm and left leg, and reciprocally.

Genuine service could be rendered by this inexpensive and very rapid apparatus. There was scarcely any cost of maintenance, and one man could easily remove the machine from the track in order to let a train pass, and afterward replace it on the rails.

It was not, however, a real innovation, since almost from the inception of cycling it was understood that railways were the most practical, the surest, and the best-rolling roadway. The *Albany Courier* in 1869 reported that on the banks of the Mohawk two landowners had constructed for themselves, in order to visit their possessions, small cars that they actuated by their arms and legs on the railways.

A fit of jealousy prompted them to initiate their own small war. One evening the two inventors ran into each other on an embankment 100 feet in height, in a sort of Yankee duel. The cars were smashed and one of the duelists was killed outright.

In Paris in 1887, military engineers tried a railway quadricycle on a line near Villette. A speed of 18 miles per hour was obtained, but the apparatus weighed 198 pounds, and for this reason was abandoned.

With the advent of the telegraph and telephone, the bicycle was almost abandoned for message-carrying purposes. However, there was still a problem for armies operating on a base apart from a commercial telegraph system.

Special attention to the problem was given by the Signal Corps of the United States Army to provide temporary telegraphic or telephonic intercommunication. Flying telegraph trains equipped with the most modern appliances of the time were located at several government stations in the West. Experiments were made pertaining to insulators, wire, batteries, and the naked-wire telephone.

The question of reeling out and recovering wire and outpost cable by bicycle, automatically, came in for a share of the attention, and the results were very satisfactory. The Signal Corps had a bicycle equipped with an automatic reel that worked perfectly. The attachment was made in San Antonio, Texas, under the supervision of its inventor, Captain R. E. Thompson of the Signal Corps. The line was laid out and recovered at a moderate rate on the day of the first test. The speed was gradually increased, and it was found that the wire could be paid out quickly. After dismounting a moment to reverse the action, the officer began a return trip, keeping in the middle of the road and riding hard. The recovery was perfectly made, the wire spooling evenly and the tension at no time troublesome, although the course of the line was occasionally departed from by many feet. This was compensated for by increasing the bulk of the spool. One third of a mile of cable could be run out, then the reel picked up, in about two minutes.

About the same time, a German living in London named Leo Kamm presented a device for the same purpose. It was a cycle for laying wires for military purposes, and consisted of an ordinary pneumatic-tired safety cycle provided with two or three drums of wire of about four inches in diameter. On each of the spools was wound a twisted wire composed of fine steel threads. Each reel carried a mile of wire. The wire passed over a wheel connected with a telegraph receiver. As the rider traveled, the rota-

Telegraph Laying Cycle (Scientific American, 8/29/96)

tion of the bicycle unwound the wire from the drum, leaving it on the ground. A bell rang before the wire was entirely paid out from the drum. When it was desired to send a message to the starting point, the rider dismounted and fixed an earth rod in the ground which was carried for that purpose. The apparatus for laying the wire weighed 7 pounds, and each mile of wire weighed 10 pounds. It was successfully used by the English army on several occasions.

In 1901 the war in South Africa brought electrical engineers into prominence by the role they played in many military operations. They needed special equipment, however, including traction engines, dynamos, arc and search lights, and twenty bicycles provided with reels for paying out telephone wire. Their first work was to install a temporary electric-light installation on the Bethulie road bridge. Six arc lights were operated by current from a dynamo driven by a traction engine. The field telephone was first put into use across this bridge, and was also used to maintain communication with the flying column, with copper wire being used. The freight yard and locomotive shops at Bloemfontein were lighted with arc and incandescent lamps. Search lights were used for various purposes, telegraphic communication was restored, and the wire-laying bicycles used in many ways.

The reel could be carried either on the frame of the machine or the back of the rider. Normally the wire was paid out directly on the ground, but for more permanent use it was supported by posts.

With bicycles firmly established as vehicles of war, new innovations were constantly being made. The United States Army had a tandem bicycle, one of the Pope Company's regular models taken directly from stock and finished plainly in enamel and nickel. On the front handlebars two army overcoats were strapped, and on the rear bars a pair of blankets. Resting safely in brackets on either side of the machine was a twelve shot repeating rifle, and hanging on each seat post a Colt quick action revolver of the latest pattern. In addition to this there was a case of signal flags extending almost the whole length of the machine, but not interfering with the riders in the least. This was the case with all the equipments, being as well and safely placed, ready for use in a moment, and yet causing not the slightest interference.

A Colt automatic gun mounted on a regular bicycle was another vehicle purchased by the gov-

Paying out Telephone Wire in South Africa (Scientific American, *1/26/01*)

New Army Tandem Bicycle (Scientific American, *2/8/96*)

ernment. The gun weighed between 39 and 40 pounds, shot 250 or 500 times—being automatically fed—and was remarkably accurate. It was fastened securely to the head of the machine, could be easily directed at any angle, and did not interfere with the rider or affect the steering of the machine. Both vehicles were as perfectly equipped with the necessary accoutrements of war as was possible at the time.

By 1900, the bicycle as a supplementary fighting unit was making headway in the various armies of the world. For years it had been regarded more as a toy than as an efficient mount, but once its capabilities were recognized, it became an integral part of the battlefield. It was noiseless, occupied small space, and consequently offered but a very insignificant target to the rifle fire of the foe. The bicycle offered great mobility and was absolutely reliable.

New Army Bicycle Mounted with a Colt Machine Gun (Scientific American, *2/8/96*)

The Dursley-Pedersen Military Cycle, Showing Principle of Construction of Front Forks (Scientific American, *10/20/00*)

England had an army of cyclists numbering about 2,000 men, all trained to repel the advance of an invading army until the main army could arrive and fight a pitched battle. Other nations were equally zealous in including the cycle into their armies. France, Germany, Italy, Belgium, and Russia all possessed military cycling detachments, and the Japanese were not long in following suit.

In the majority of cases, however, the cycle generally used was of a collapsible design. The machine was so constructed that it could be folded up into a small package and slung on the back of the rider out of the way. To satisfactorily accomplish this with the then existing machine was a very difficult matter. The majority of the devices by which the cycle could be folded were based on the idea of hinging the frame in some manner. This principle, however, destroyed the rigidity and strength of the machine to a very appreciable degree.

Then a military cycle was devised which was said to be stronger, more rigid and lighter than the conventional type of machine. Lightness commensurate with strength and rigidity in a military cycle was a great recommendation toward its utility on the battlefield.

The frame was constructed on the system of triangles, the principle that was most conducive to stability. The tubes of the frame were doubled throughout, whereas in the existing type of cycle they were single. A very important improvement was the front section of the frame, which carried the steering wheel. There was no fork. This was one of the most serious defects inherent in the diamond frame, since the system of triangles had to be abandoned somewhat in the front head. But in the Dursley-Pedersen, as the new cycle was known, this defect was overcome. There were a pair of tubes springing from the hub of the front wheel on either side to the head of the frame. The front tubes on each side were perfectly straight, but the second tubes were drawn back in the center, and an open steel crown plate held all four in position. From the head of the machine the tubes dropping to the crank bracket were placed almost vertically, while from the crank bracket two more tubes sprang to the front fork, holding it firmly in position. From the head also dropped the tubes to the hub of the back wheel, and another pair of tubes radiated from the crank bracket to carry the saddle, which was one of the most conspicuous features of the whole machine. It was a seat suspended hammock fashion between seven spiral springs attached to the adjustable saddle pillar and the top front fork, to which it was secured by means of a strap, which could be adjusted so as to tighten or to slacken the saddle as desired. This unique saddle adjusted itself to every movement of the body, and allowed perfect freedom to those muscles which cycling brought into play. By this means perineal pressure was entirely averted, while perfect ventilation, ease, comfort, and softness of seat were assured. As the strain between the saddle pillar and the hub of the back wheel was purely tensile, they were connected on each side by wires in place of tubes. The

Bicycle Folded and Carried on Rider's Back (Scientific American, *10/20/00*)

steel throughout, was only 15 pounds. It folded up so compactly that one could climb obstructions and perform the ordinary military duties with the greatest facility and without the slightest inconvenience. The rifle was fixed vertically in a slot on the frame of the front wheel.

Even after the automobile made its appearance in Europe the bicycle was still preferred for many army uses. For scouting and the conveyance of dispatches, the bicycle was without rival, being noiseless, occupying small space and affording a very small target. It was reliable, and a bicycle division very mobile. Also, the wheel required no forage supplies.

The French army had a wheel invented by Captain Gerard which could be folded up and carried on the back. The frame was strengthened by a second tube running parallel with the first, thus giving the machine great rigidity. These two tubes, because of their considerable diameter, reduced the vibration that used up so much of the rider's energy. At the center of the right-hand side of the parallelogram forming the frame, there was a ball joint. Each of the parallel tubes was divided in the center, and the ends, which were beveled, were

joining of the tubes throughout the machine was accomplished by sweating instead of the more general brazing, the former method considered to be stronger. The handlebar was passed through the front tubes and fixed at a low elevation, the handles curving upward to the desired height.

Some idea of the strength of the principle of construction may be gathered from the fact that the inventor's original machine was built of poplar sticks instead of steel tubes, secured together with twine, and represented a total weight of 18 pounds. The machine, primitive though its construction was, had been ridden no less than 5,000 miles without the slightest mishap.

The cycle was folded by slipping out the front wheel and tubes at the head and at the point where the two tubes radiating from the crank bracket joined the front tubes. The front wheel then folded back upon the back wheel and was kept in position with a strap. It took only twenty seconds to perform the operation and to sling it on one's back, and it could as readily be put together again. The total weight of the machine, which was constructed of

Folding Bicycle, with Rifle Attached, Weight 15 Pounds (Scientific American, *10/20/00*)

French Military Folding Bicycle (Scientific American, *10/26/01*)

held in place, when the machine was opened, by coupling sockets. When the ends of the tubes were exposed by loosening the sockets and shoving them back upon the rings, the front part of the bicycle could be folded around onto the rear half, the wheels being superimposed. If desired, the bicycle could be divided into two parts, while the handlebar could be removed from the steering head. A

The Automobile for Military Instruction (Scientific American, *9/27/02*)

novel form of brake was also provided. The wheel was of such a height that the bicyclist could maintain such a position in the saddle that he could at any moment touch the ground with his feet.

The use of the automobile in connection with military service for mounting light artillery began with Major R. P. Davidson, commandant at the Northwestern Military Academy of Highland Park, Illinois. The major had experimented with motor vehicles for several years, in making forced marches, long-distance tours, and in what might be called light artillery evolutions. The wretched road conditions brought him to the conclusion that the automobile alone was not sufficient for the job.

In 1902 the cadet corps of the academy was organized to include a bicycle and automobile gun attachment, which was probably the only military organization of its kind in the world. The gun battery consisted of two Colt automatic rapid-fire pieces of 7 millimeters caliber, each firing 480 shots per minute. They were constructed to utilize smokeless powder, and each was equipped with a bullet shield to protect the operator when in action. Each gun was manned by a sergeant and three privates armed with revolvers. The motor vehicles were operated by 10-horsepower engines utilizing gasoline, giving a speed of 25 miles an hour on the ordinary country pike. The carriages had reservoirs with a capacity for 22 gallons of gasoline, and were equipped with acetylene lamps for night service.

The front portion of the motor contained a foundation of sheet steel upon which the gun was mounted. The general design of the carriage was conceived by Major Davidson after much experimentation.

The gun squad accompanied the bicycle infantry as in the accompanying photograph in marches through northern Illinois. To test the cross-country ability of the vehicles, trips were frequently taken through cultivated fields and underbrush, the idea being to test the efficacy of the carriages as a substitute for horses in artillery service.

In 1906 a very convenient type of portable wireless telegraph station was constructed by the Wireless Telegraph Company of Berlin of such lightness it required no cart to transport.

Chiefly remarkable in this portable outfit was the means of generating energy. A bicycle dynamo was used, the constructive principle of which was simple. A small direct-current dynamo of about 100 watts' output was fitted to a bicycle frame. The rider kept the machine going by smart pedaling. From the sprocket of the bicycle frame the movement was transmitted to the dynamo by means of a belt, driving a specially designed aluminum disk, the ratio of transmission being so designed as to have the dynamo produce sparks of 4 millimeters'

length in the induction coil, in normal operation. As the dynamo was located in front of the operator, the latter was in a position at any moment to supervise its uniform activity. The weight of the dynamo outfit was 66 pounds.

In place of this device, a stationary motorcycle with a dynamo fitted on could be used, or a portable accumulator battery could supply the energy required.

Other inventors in the world were working on like projects. A compact wireless telegraphic plant of the portable type was constructed by Sir Oliver Lodge and Dr. Alexander Muirhead. The installa-

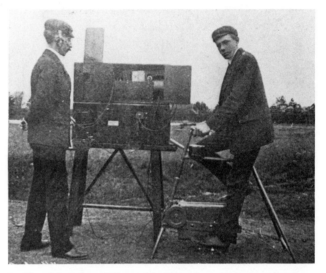

Lodge-Muirhead Portable Wireless Telegraph Plant for military use. The current is generated by a small continuous-current motor driven from a stationary bicycle. (Scientific American, 9/22/06)

A bicycle generating station used by the German army's wireless telegraph corps in the South African campaign (Scientific American, 1/13/06)

tion, which was self-contained, was especially intended for military operations, and for facilitating transport over difficult country it was made as light and compact as possible. It could be easily stowed and carried by mule. It had sufficient capacity to establish communication over distances up to 50 miles across land or 150 miles over sea.

The antennae were carried by bamboo poles, of short, convenient lengths for transport, which poles, when fitted together, formed a somewhat cubical structure 40 feet in height. No earth capacity was needed, and in fact was avoided to insure the greatest degree of efficiency over long distances.

The transmitting and receiving installations were

carried in a small cabinet and occupied the main space. When in use, this cabinet was supported upon a folding trestle. The necessary current was generated by means of a small continuous-current dynamo carried in a frame resembling that of a bicycle, the power being supplied by bicycle pedal action, with the electric valve system devised by Sir Oliver to accumulate the impulses. For receiving messages the Lodge vibrating needlepoint-oil-mercury coherer with telephone receiver was fitted.

In one form or another, the bicycle remained in favor with the armies of the world until the motorcycle became its replacement.

10

A Bicycle Factory

THE DEMAND FOR BICYCLES WAS SO GREAT IT helped pioneer the assembly-line system used in modern factories. In 1891 the Overman Wheel Co., in Chicopee Falls, Massachusetts, where Victor bicycles were manufactured, was a prime example. It occupied two extensive buildings on opposite sides of the street that were connected by a bridge. The first of these buildings, while in process of construction, was supposed to be large enough to meet the demands of the business for many years, but before the structure was completed it was determined that the works must be doubled, and, as a consequence, a second building was planned and proceeded with as rapidly as possible. These buildings were made of brick with granite trimmings; the piers between the walls that supported the floors were brick, with granite binders and iron caps. The floors were made of heavy matched pine plank having a thickness of 2½ inches, covered with diagonal pine flooring, on the top of which was placed a floor of hard maple. The ceilings and timbers were covered with asbestos and tin, thus rendering the wooden portions practically fireproof.

The success of this concern was due in no small degree to Mr. Overman's genius in planning, building, and equipping his own shop. The growth of the business was such that in a short time both of the big buildings, with all the machinery and appliances contained in them, were scarcely able to keep up with the demands of the business, even when work was carried on night and day, as it was in the busy season. Each building was provided with a pair of 100-horsepower engines and boilers to match, and the works were so constructed that all the machinery in both buildings could be driven by either set of engines.

The machinery used was the best that money could buy or genius devise, and as soon as the need developed for other type machinery, it was purchased or constructed and set at work as soon as possible. Everything that was used in the construction of the Victor machines, with the exception of the rubber tires, was made on the premises by day labor. No contract labor was allowed, and, as a rule, no workman under twenty years was employed, it having been found by experience that boys were apt to be not sufficiently alive to the importance of always doing their best work to justify their employment. All the workmen here employed were skilled mechanics and also stood high as citizens, as the Overman Wheel Company would not employ an individual who disgraced himself, whether in the works or out.

General View of the Works at Chicopee Falls, Mass (Scientific American, 5/2/91)

As the machines were made entirely of steel, it was obvious that drop forging be used largely in the process of construction, and the forges in the shop were constructed double throughout for the purpose of adapting them to the use of liquid or solid fuel. Crude petroleum was the standard fuel for heating the steel. It was atomized and blown into

Assembling the Victor Bicycles (Scientific American, 5/2/91)

the forges by air under pressure. The petroleum for this purpose was taken through a private pipeline from tank cars at the railway, and stored in an underground reservoir having a capacity of several carloads. Petroleum was used under the boilers and in the hardening furnaces, and all these furnaces were so arranged that should the supply of petroleum fail, even temporarily, the coal furnaces could be immediately started and work proceed without interruption. Besides the petroleum heating furnaces there were gas blowpipes, and furnaces supplied with gas from a private plant.

A separate screw machine room was maintained since the parts of the machines were held together mainly by screws, screw threads and nuts, and a great deal of fine machinery was required to accomplish this part of the work. Most parts were carefully nickel plated in preference to japanning, or any other finish. After plating in the separate department used for this job, the parts were conveyed to the buffing room.

The parts of the wheels were put together and the wheels were trued and adjusted in a department devoted to that purpose, and one of the floors

Drop-Forging Shop (Scientific American, 5/2/91)

Wheel Making (Scientific American, 5/2/91)

was used for assembling the parts of the machine. After assembling, the machines were all tested. At first the machines were tested on the road, but the uncertainty of the weather made it necessary to provide a place under shelter, so the upper story of the newer building was provided with a floor especially prepared for this purpose, the floor having pavements representing all kinds of roads, so that the behavior of the wheels on the different roads could be readily studied.

The tools used in the different departments of the establishment were kept in a fireproof vault in charge of competent attendants. They were made in triplicate and given out according to a regular system.

The illumination of the building was accomplished by an electric light plant having a capacity for 1,000 16-candlepower lamps. The protection against the fire was very complete, the works having a water tower on the roof, an underground reservoir with a capacity of 30,000 gallons, and a standpipe from the city works on every floor.

The works employed 600 men in 1891, and it soon grew to a thousand.

The office where the president presided was the hub of this enterprise. Every department was made to report itself through the medium of an electrical apparatus in the office. The pressure of the steam in the boilers, the temperature of the japanning ovens, the level of the water in the water reservoir, were all made to report automatically at the office. Here, also, was the master clock which controlled the secondary clocks throughout the factory, and connected with this clock was an engineer's signal for blowing the whistle, the signals for the closing of the gates, etc.

The capital stock of the Overman Wheel Company was $250,000, with a surplus of a like amount. The president of the company was A. H. Overman, of Springfield, the treasurer, E. S. White. Branch houses were established at Boston, Washington, Denver, and San Francisco, where customers could make precisely the same business arrangements as at the home office.

Several varieties of bicycles were made at Overman's, but the model C was the kind commonly known as the "safety," both wheels being of ap-

Screw-Machine Room (Scientific American, 5/2/91)

proximately the same diameter. The machine had a very rigid frame of diamond shape; the rear or driving wheel was furnished with what is known as the Victor cushion tire, which was a simple arch of rubber extending from edge to edge of the rim. Its side walls were held against spreading by side flanges having rounded edges which the tire covered and protected. The base of the tire rested on a horizontal rim bed which aided materially in giving lateral stiffness to the tire and strength to the hollow rim. With this construction the rubber displaced inwardly under pressure, and the movement of the rubber was almost entirely in a radial direction, a fact which accounts for the great elasticity of the Victor cushion tire.

The elasticity of the forward part of the machine was secured by the Victor spring fork, which proved to be a device of great value. In connection with the cushion tire, it insured a smooth and steady action. The machine was provided throughout with the finest ball bearings, and the pedals were made on a new plan original with the Overman Wheel Co. Being rectangular in section, they automatically adjusted themselves to the curve of the boot and gave a good bearing to the sole of the foot.

The Victor Bicycle (Scientific American, 5/2/91)

11

Early Mopeds

FROM THE TIME THE VELOCIPEDE ACHIEVED popularity, inventors were determined to power it by something other than human exertion. As early as 1868 W. W. Austin of Winthrop, Massachusetts, attached a coal-burning steam engine to his velocipede. The piston rods were connected to cranks on the rear wheel, and the boiler was hung amidships and directly back of the saddle. This vehicle, which naturally had a very limited steaming radius, was the forerunner of the large family of mopeds and motorcycles now in existence. It was crude and ungainly and had painfully narrow limitations, but its builder solemnly swore he'd ridden it over 2,000 miles. Whether the extreme proximity of the boiler and smokestack to the rider's anatomy seriously diluted his enjoyment of his weird vehicle, history does not state.

In 1869 another version appeared. The cylinders and their attachments to the two driving wheels are not shown in the engraving, but they were placed vertically in front of the boiler, between it and the seat, and connected with cranks on the shaft of the driving wheels. The engraving shows the position of the boiler relative to the other parts of the machine. The engine was a direct-acting compound engine of two cylinders, each cylinder 2½ inches in diameter and with a 5-inch stroke. The steering gear consisted of an endless chain over a grooved wheel, fixed between the forked shaft just over the front wheel. This arrangement gave power to the front wheel, so that in turning a corner, this wheel took a wider sweep than the two driving wheels, which went first. In traveling on a straight road (backwards) the machine was turned to either side by turning the steering wheel to the opposite side. The boiler was a vertical one, with four tubes of 1½-inch internal diameter, hanging down by the side of the firebox. The firegate was cast with four holes in it to receive the bottom ends of the tubes, so as to help hold them firmly. Its dimensions were:

Austin Steam Velocipede (Scientific American, 7/5/13)

91

Steam Velocipede (Scientific American, *2/13/69*)

"Highflyer" 1876 (Scientific American, *7/5/13*)

height of boiler, 2 feet, 6 inches; height of firebox, 15 inches; diameter of firebox, 11 inches; diameter of boiler, 14 inches. The firebox and tubes were copper, pressure 200 pounds, but 25 pounds of steam would be equal to a velocipede propelled by the feet. Great speed was expected from this velocipede, but it never really caught on.

In 1876 the English exhibited a curious vehicle, the "Highflyer" as it was named. It was a velocipede tricycle equipped with two small engines fitted to the interior of the front fork. Over the rear wheels was supported a little copper boiler and petroleum furnace. The steam was carried from the boiler to the engines through the frame of the machine and regulated by a turn-cock placed conveniently to the operator. The driving rods communicated with the cranks on the main axle. The Highflyer had one large driving wheel in front, and two small balance wheels in the rear.

In 1872 Louis Perreaux patented improvements on a velocipede, and in 1880 he added a steam-powering device and exhibited his machine at the Industrial Exhibition at the Champs Elysées in Paris. The generator, the fireplace, and the motor were arranged behind the saddle of the velocipede, after the manner of the portmanteau of a horseman. Chains or belts transmitted motion from the engine to the wheels. All the parts were small, well put together, and very compact. The small tubular boiler was cylindrical and had a capacity of about 3 quarts. At the sides were two receptacles containing a sufficient supply of water to last during a journey of two to three hours. The piston of th engine was about one inch in diameter and had 3-inch stroke. The whole engine was a mere plaything, and yet, with a pressure of three and one-half

atmospheres, it had sufficient power to drive the velocipede at a speed of from 15 to 18 miles per hour. The fireplace that heated the boiler was an ingenious novelty, and consisted of a small gasometer fed by wood spirits. The vapor of the alcohol issued through holes, and gave a flame of great calorific power. The fire was lighted at will, the steam up in a matter of minutes. A method was provided for regulating the escape of the alcohol vapor, and consequently the intensity of the heat. Externally the boiler was furnished with two tubes rolled in the form of a spiral, so the steam which was produced circulated through them continuously, and was exposed directly to the fire before entering the motor. The steam being superheated, no water was carried over with it. With a speed of eighteen miles an hour, the cost of alcohol con-

Steam Velocipede (Scientific American, *2/21/80*)

sumed was from 40 to 60 cents (this calculation for France). It wasn't very economical, but it was pleasant to have a horse under control that ate only when he worked.

In 1882 Sir Thomas Parkyns invented a steam tricycle that he called the "Baronet." The apparatus consisted of an ordinary tricycle, to which was adapted a small tubular boiler placed horizontally a little to the rear of the seat, between the two large wheels, and which was heated with petroleum; of a water reservoir, which served at the same time for condensation by means of a worm; and of a cylinder with truck actuating three gearings, which, in controlling one another, gave motion to the wheels of the tricycle. The apparatus was arranged so as to be actuated with the feet alone, with the engine alone, or by the combined action of the feet and engine. Moreover, it required the action of the feet to start the tricycle going.

Messrs. Bateman & Co., of Greenwich, who were commissioned by Sir Parkyns to construct his steam tricycle for sale, were obliged to modify the whole structure before offering it to the public. The inventor, although he possessed excellent ideas, was lacking in the special knowledge necessary for the construction of a machine practically adapted for working.

These engineers began by modifying the form of certain parts and strengthening them, and by replacing the horizontal boiler with a recently invented very powerful rotary motor. The original machine could scarcely exceed a speed of 7 to 9 miles per hour, but the new manufacturers gave it a speed of 13 miles, and also the power to ascend certain grades, as well as making it unnecessary to use the feet. They kept the mode of heating by petroleum as it had the advantage of giving a fire easy to keep up, of giving out no smoke, and of permitting a large amount of fuel to be carried within little space.

However, the manufacturers limited the amount of time they gave to the new vehicle because of a law in England forbidding the use of any steam motor on the streets unless it was preceded by a person on foot and run at a maximum speed of three miles per hour.

Another original motorcycle was a steam machine devised in 1884 by L. D. and W. E. Copeland, two California experimenters. The engine and boiler formed a compact and ingenious invention that, inclusive of the driving pulley, weighed but 16 ounces. This undoubtedly was the first application of the belt drive to a motorcycle.

In a description of this machine in a cycling journal of that period a writer said, "The speed of the pulley is seven revolutions a minute. Enough water can be taken into the boiler to last an hour, and the power of the engine is sufficient to drive the 51-inch bicycle about 12 miles per hour on the floor, or about one mile in eight minutes on the road; hence it will be seen that it would be quite an

Copeland Steam Machine, 1884 (Scientific American, 7/5/13)

Sir Thomas Parkyns's Steam Velocipede (Scientific American, 9/30/82)

93

assistance to the feet in propelling the machine. By unscrewing a couple of bolts the engine can be removed, when there remains a bicycle pure and simple."

The engine of this machine was attached to a lever-drive high-wheel bicycle, and could readily be removed from it. After exhibiting the machine throughout California, one of the Copeland brothers came east with it and interested a prominent bicycle manufacturer. The latter sought to improve it by employing a more powerful engine and adapting it to a three-wheeled vehicle. Several steam tricycles were constructed by Copeland himself, who remained in the East quite a time in the hope of seeing the manufacture of his machine begun. Although his machines appeared to operate satisfactorily, the public had not become quite ready to accept such a radical departure and notable advancement in transportation facilities, and the machines soon were lost sight of, to remain dear only to the memories of the builders and a few other enthusiasts of those days. Like many other inventors, the Copelands and their motorcycles were far ahead of the time, and their worth was unappreciated.

Inventors had been experimenting with steam power in vehicles since 1680 when Sir Isaac Newton devised the first steam carriage, but although many were tried after the velocipede became popular and before, none is even remembered today. It was left to an unknown German, Gottlieb Daimler, to produce the first gasoline-engined bicycle.

Daimler's machine was put together around 1885, but not patented in this country until January 17, 1888. Its most interesting feature was the upright position of its engine and its belt drive to the rear wheel. Though the frame of the machine was of

Daimler's Motorcycle of 1885 (Scientific American, 7/5/13)

Twombley's Machine of 1895 (Scientific American, 7/5/13)

Sir Isaac Newton's Steam Carriage of 1680 (Scientific American, 1/22/87)

wooden construction and fitted with iron-tired wheels, such modern features as handlebar steering, twist-grip-operated brake, and saddle over the engine were present. In the second version, which was ridden in 1886, the engine drive to the rear wheel was by way of a countershaft, pinion, and internally toothed gear ring.

As was the way with inventors, others were working on the same problem, and without any knowledge of Daimler's efforts. It was the luck of history that made Daimler known as the father of the motorcycle.

Among the many petroleum-powered machines that appeared on the scene was the petroleum tricycle designed by M. De Dion and Bouton, well-known builders of automobile carriages. When fully equipped, it weighed 88 pounds. In addition

Volta's Steamer, 1895 (Scientific American, 7/5/13)

Roper's Machine, 1896 (Scientific American, 7/5/13)

A Petroleum Tricycle (Scientific American, 6/8/95)

to the motor, there were pedals for actuating the machine through the medium of sprocket wheels and a chain. The tricycle was started, after mounting, by giving the pedals a few turns until the motor began to operate. Then the pedals ceased to be used, and the rider need only steer the machine. In climbing hills the pedals were sometimes used as an auxiliary force. This combination of mechanical and human power permitted the rider to enjoy the pleasures of locomotion without the aid of the motor or to economize the combustible when necessary.

The motor was not complicated. It was actuated by the explosion of a mixture of air and the vapor of the petroleum. The explosion was effected by means of electricity. The motor was one-third of a horse power, the shaft making 800 turns per minute. With the help of the motor and pedals it was possible to attain a speed of 18 miles an hour. The carburetor had been dispensed with, its place being

taken by a small pump, which was actuated slowly by the motor and thus utilized the petroleum drop by drop. The clumsy and heavy water jacket had also been eliminated, the cylinder being cooled by contact with the air.

A small satchel resembling a photographic camera was fixed to the frame in front. This satchel carried a dry battery that would run the exploder for one hundred hours. It was connected with a spark coil by means of insulated cord. The rider could stop the motor instantly by cutting off the current with a switch.

A larger model surfaced in California, built to order by A. Schilling and Sons. It combined a wagon with the tricycle, and was propelled by a 2-horsepower Golden Gate balanced engine. The machine was made to carry three persons on the

Gas Engine Tricycle (Scientific American, 1/12/95)

single broad seat, though operated by one, with surplus power sufficient to trail one or two buggies or a loaded wagon, depending on the road. It carried 12 hours' supply of gasoline, or 2½ gallons, and could easily attain a speed of from 10 to 12 miles per hour on a good road. It was geared in such a manner that the movement of a lever increased or decreased the speed, enabling the driver to climb grades of considerable pitch.

It was quite safe and was simple in construction, the design of the inventor being to have as few pieces and parts as possible. The wheels and frame supporting the engine were strong and the entire machine was constructed to withstand hard usage.

In the latter part of 1894 the National Bicycle Exhibition was held for a week at Madison Square Garden in New York, and the industry went all out for the show. Just inside the entrance an electric bicycle high on the wall could be seen at night with its wheels and gears in motion, and studded with electric lamps. It was about 20 feet long and 13 feet high, with 8-foot wheels. Some 2,200 lamps were used to light it up.

There were 163 exhibitors who showed their wheels in enclosed spaces around the floor, while on a large stage at one side trick riding and other performances were given while a band provided music. The exhibits were mounted on high standards so they could be examined without stooping when they weren't in operation in the hall. There were so many novelties in construction of pedals, cranks, hubs, handlebars and other details that it

The National Bicycle Exhibition in Madison Square Garden, New York—General View (Scientific American, 2/9/95)

was difficult to see them all. There were four-wheelers, tricycles, two-wheelers, tandems, children's models, and the new lightweight cycles weighing only 8 or 9 pounds.

There were motorized versions galore, but human-powered bicycles still dominated the scene, and it would be a while before the motorcycle really came into its own.

Most people used their wheels largely for exercise and anything in the way of power propulsion would defeat this purpose. However, there were people who welcomed the practical motorcycle since it would enable them to prolong their excursions and eliminate the element of fatigue.

In 1896 Nelson S. Hopkins of Williamsville, New York, built an experimental motorcycle. The first motor weighed 12 pounds, but then the inventor succeeded in building a motor which would propel a wheel and rider over moderate grades that weighed only 8½ pounds.

The motive power was derived from gasoline contained in an aluminum reservoir strapped to the upper part of the diamond frame. From the reservoir the gasoline was conveyed to the carburetor by means of a small pipe. A valve limited the quantity of the fuel that was admitted to the carburetor. This valve could be operated from the saddle by means of a rod, stopped and started the motor, and regulated the speed. From the carburetor, where the vapor of the gasoline had been mixed with air, the mixture was drawn into the compressor and was then forced into one of the two explosion cylinders where the charge was ignited by an electric spark, contact being controlled by the movement of the piston. The use of two cylinders made it possible to obtain an impulse at every turn of the shaft and by means of gears the wheel was propelled with great freedom from jerkiness and vibration. The battery was placed under the saddle in a tool bag, and the spark coil was fastened to the diamond frame, but later both battery and coil were carried in the tool bag.

At the back of the shaft was a small steel gear wheel that ran with a larger one of phosphor bronze secured to the hub of the wheel. This large gear wheel was movable, and it was arranged so that the motor could be entirely disconnected from the running gear, thus allowing the wheel to be propelled in the ordinary manner. The feet rested on coasters or on the pedals. Usually the chain was thrown out of gear by the aid of the clutch, but in

The Motorcycle (Scientific American, 2/9/95)

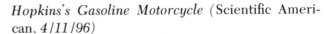

Hopkins's Gasoline Motorcycle (Scientific American, 4/11/96)

hill climbing both the motor and pedals were used to propel the bicycle.

It was pointed out that the wheel was impossible to run without a rider to keep it balanced and that, should he fall, the wheel would stop of its own accord. The weight of the motor was on one side, which tended to throw the wheel out of balance, but this was remedied by throwing the center of the saddle over a trifle. All working parts, except the gears, were inclosed.

At the same time a benzine-fueled machine made in Munich was brought to this country. The frame

97

of the machine was formed of four parallel tubes, two on either side, connected with the main journal boxes of the rear or drive wheel, and united at their forward ends with two pairs of oblique tubes connected by cross bars at the top, and carrying the steering head which held the shank of the front fork as in an ordinary bicycle.

Between the two pairs of horizontal bars were secured two motor cylinders, formed in one casting and provided with a water jacket. The cylinders contained pistons connected by piston rods with the crank on the main shaft. The bearings of the crank pins, as well as the bearings of the main shaft, were rendered nearly frictionless by the use of balls, as in the bearings of an ordinary bicycle. The cylinders were single acting, and the cranks, which were on opposite sides of the rear wheel, were parallel and extended in the same direction. The engines worked on the four-cycle principle and were so timed as to give one effective impulse for each revolution of the drive wheel.

On top of the cylinder, above the explosion chamber at the rear of the piston, was a valve chest containing two pairs of poppet valves, one pair to each cylinder. The valve chest was furnished with two separate chambers, one for the supply of the explosive mixture, the other for the escape of the exhaust. The valves were held to their seats by spiral springs surrounding their stems. The valves that admitted the explosive mixture were provided with light springs, so that when the pistons moved forward the valves opened inward automatically. But the exhaust valves were furnished with heavier springs, which held them to their seats at all times except when they were depressed by the valve operating levers.

These levers were made to open their respective valves in alternation by a combination of levers. On the side of the rear or drive wheel a cam was secured on which pressed a roller, carried by the arm, jointed to the lower side bar. A rod connected with the arm and was jointed to one side of the lever, the opposite of which carried the hook. To the hook was pivoted a three-armed lever which was held in frictional contact with the hook by a strong spiral spring.

Pivoted to the top of the cylinders were two arms which were pressed toward the center of the cylinder to springs. The forward projecting arm of the lever was capable of bearing against the free end of one or the other of the arms. The shorter arms of

Side View of Motorcycle Partly in Section (Scientific American, *12/12/96*)

Valve Motion of Motorcycle (Scientific American, *12/12/96*)

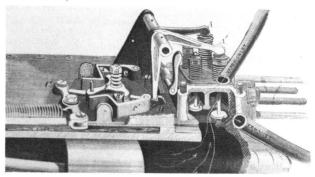

the lever were alternately brought into engagement with studs projecting from the top of the cylinders. The angled arms were pivoted on a rod supported by ears projecting from the cylinders, and their downwardly projecting ends were engaged in alternation by the hook. This action of the exhaust mechanism controlled the machine.

The ignition of the charge was effected by heating the nickel tubes projecting about 2½ inches from the rear ends of the cylinders into the ignition box. In the box was a vapor burner that received its vapor from the vertical tube beside the box. It contained a wick saturated with benzine from the reservoir. The tubes extended into a fireclay chamber with three nickel spirals below the tubes for distributing and retaining the heat. The heating burner heated both nickel tubes, thus insuring prompt and regular explosions. The ignition tube was clamped in place by a yoke. The lower oblique tube on one side of the machine conveyed air to the burner, and the tube on the other side served as a chimney to carry the products of combustion from the burner.

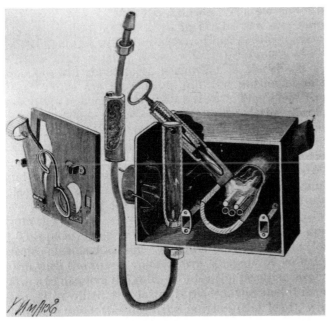

Igniting Apparatus (Scientific American, *12/12/96*)

Benzine Reservoir (Scientific American, *12/12/96*)

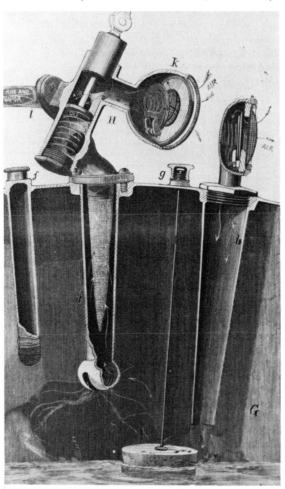

The benzine was contained in the reservoir supported by the oblique tubes at the front of the machine. This reservoir was connected directly to the burner that heated the ignition tube. The top of the reservoir held a screw-capped filling tube, the lower end of which was covered with wire gauze. A cork float attached to a nipple on the top showed the depth of the liquid in the reservoir.

A conical air-supply tube projected into the reservoir. It had a check valve to keep the tube closed except when a partial vacuum was formed through the action of the engine. The proportion of benzine vapor and air conveyed to the engine depended on the position of the valve. This was regulated by the lever pivoted to the handlebar and connected with the valve by a rod. The lever had a latch passing under a lug projecting from the handlebar when the valve was closed, and when the lever was released to open the valve, the regulating cone at the end of the lever rested against a finger projecting from the handlebar and served to adjust the position of the valve by engagement with the finger as it screwed along the threaded end of the lever.

The exhaust was taken to a hood made in the form of a hollow quarter cylinder, which was divided into two compartments by a perforated curved partition. The exhaust pipe entered the smaller compartment and the larger compartment was filled with asbestos cord. The asbestos cord served as a muffler to deaden the noise of the exhaust.

A curved water tank was attached over the drive wheel, connected with the water jacket around the cylinders, and the circulation of the water prevented the overheating of the cylinders. The oil for the lubrication of the cylinders was contained in the upper oblique tube, and fed to the cylinders by a sight feed.

To start the motorcycle, the reservoir was partly filled with benzine, the door at the back of the ignition box opened and the burner for heating the ignition tube was started by giving it a preliminary heating with an alcohol torch. As the door of the ignition box opened for this purpose, the air-supply pipe closed automatically. When the tubes were red hot, the valve opened and the machine was moved forward by the operator until an explosion occurred. Then he mounted the machine and rode on his way. By manipulating the hand lever, the supply of explosive mixture, and consequently the speed of the machine, was regulated.

The action of the machine was novel. The forward motion of the piston drew in the explosive mixture through a valve, and on its return compressed the mixture in the explosion chamber behind the piston. A portion of the mixture was forced into the hot tube, where it was ignited, forcing the piston outwardly to give the propelling impulse. The return stroke of the piston expelled the products of combustion through the exhaust valve, which was opened by the cam at the proper moment through the use of the roller and hook. The cylinders operated alternately, thereby giving one effective impulse for each revolution of the drive wheel. To stop the machine, it was only necessary to close the valve and apply the brakes.

The engine cylinders were $3^9/_{16}$ inches in diameter, with a stroke of $4^5/_8$ inches. The supply- and exhaust-valve apertures were ½ inch in diameter. The benzine reservoir was 13 inches long and 7½ inches in diameter. The driving wheel was 22 inches in diameter and the guiding wheel 26 inches in diameter. The pneumatic tires were made specially large and heavy to support the weight of the rider and machine. The tread of the machine was 4 feet, the weight when in running order 115 pounds. The reservoir contained a supply of benzine sufficent for a run of 12 hours. The machine could run at a speed of from 3 to 24 miles per hour, depending on the road.

Man's inventiveness was at full swing around the turn of the century, and the patent office worked overtime to keep up with the demand.

A mechanic named Steffey, from San Diego, California, invented a particularly lightweight machine simply by contriving a motor attachment for existing bicycles. It consisted of a small, water-jacketed motor. On one side was the flywheel, and on the other a small sprocket which connected to a large auxiliary driving sprocket on the back wheel by a chain passing over a sprocket guide wheel supported on the bicycle frame. The tank, 1, contained the gasoline, while in the box, 2, was the ignition battery. This was connected by flexible cord to the igniter of the motor and to a push button, 6, located under one of the handles of the handlebar. The motor was lubricated from the oil cup, 10, and was cooled by water from the tank, 7, placed under the seat which circulated through the pipes, 8, to and from the water jacket. The tube, 9, was a muffler.

The Steffey Motorcycle (Scientific American, 3/3/00)

Motor Attachment for Bicycles (Scientific American, 3/3/00)

In starting the machine, the compression lever, 4, was released, then the rider mounted and drove ahead by giving the pedals two or three revolutions in the ordinary way. He immediately threw on the compression lever, 4, and pressed the button, 6, and the motor started and drove the machine at a good rate of speed. The speed could be regulated by moving the wire hook, 5, which controlled the air mixture. The bicycle could be stopped by simply ceasing to press the igniter circuit button, causing the compression of the unexploded charges to powerfully brake the motor.

All parts of the motor were encased with remarkable compactness to fit into the front fork of the bicycle. The entire weight of the attachment was about 25 pounds, and a pint of gasoline was sufficient to drive the bicycle over 20 miles.

The Marsh Motor Bicycle was another invention that made its appearance on the market. The motor was of the four-cycle jacketless type, using gasoline as fuel. It weighed 20 pounds, and was 14 inches high by 4 inches wide. The crank case was 7 inches in diameter. The cylinder was 1⅞ inches in diameter and 2¼-inch stroke. The outside part of the crankcase was an aluminum casting, carefully machined to receive the cylinder and the side disks. The latter were made of steel and contained the bearings. This base was fitted with a filler conveniently located on the front side above the center, through which the lubricating oil was poured. It also had a drip in the bottom for draining the oil.

The cast-iron cylinder was fastened to the base with six screws. The ignition plug screwed into the combustion chamber. The upper part of the motor was fastened to a seat post by a lug fixture through which the exhaust passed on its way from the cylinder to the muffler. Directly on top of the combustion chamber was a nickel-plated induction valve, which directly under the chamber was an exhaust-valve stem and the spring which closed it. The compression-relief valve was on top of the cylinder.

On the left-hand side of the motor were the gear and cam for operating the exhaust valve and also the ignition device. These were inclosed in an oil-tight case. On the left-hand side was the sprocket which drove the rear wheel. On the left of the crankcase a flat projection was tapped to receive four 4-inch screws, which were part of the fastening that held the motor in place. The great feature of this motor was the construction of its bearings, which were so arranged that it had a large amount of bearing surface and still was less than 4 inches wide overall, which permitted it to be placed between the cranks of any ordinary road wheel.

The motor was located in the angle of the frame in front of the seat post and just above the hanger sprocket, and was fastened to it at the back of the base and also at the back of the cylinder.

The pedal side of the rear hub was fitted with a coaster brake, the motor side being fitted with a 32-tooth sprocket, 1-inch pitch, and ⅜ inch wide. The sprocket on the motor had five teeth, which allowed the same to revolve 6⅖ times to one turn of the rear wheel. As the rear wheel was 28 inches in diameter, the motor ran a little over 2,300

Motor Bicycle (Scientific American, 8/18/00)

Details of Engine (Scientific American, 8/18/00)

revolutions per minute when the cycle was making 30 miles an hour.

The valves and ignition device were correctly proportioned and carefully made, and with the chain removed from the motor, it could reach a speed of 5,000 revolutions a minute without missing an explosion. The motor chain could be adjusted by moving the rear wheel back and forth in the jaws in which it hung, while the pedal chain was adjusted by turning the eccentric around in the bottom bracket.

The cylindrical box on the forward part of the frame held the spark coil, while a tube on top of the frame just forward of the saddle, contained four cells of dry battery, which were only 1¹¹/₁₆ inches in diameter by 1⅞ inches long, and weighed complete, case and all, 1¼ pounds. A coil and set of these batteries would last nearly 500 miles, which was an item of some notice, as it saved carrying the bulky batteries ordinarily used, which weighed from 12 to 15 pounds.

The 1-quart fuel tank—enough for 100 miles—was on the rear of the saddle post. Below the fuel tank was the carburetor, which was of the vaporizing type and automatic in its operation. It could always be depended upon to give the right mixture of gas and air, and as much as the engine could use at all times. It was securely fastened to the seat mast by a lug.

At the left of the cylinder was an air scoop, which sent warm air to the carburetor. The muffler, made from brass tubing, 2 inches in diameter and 7 inches long, and lined with asbestos and perforated with a number of small holes on either side, was at the rear of the seat mast between the base of the motor and the rear wheel. It was very efficient, muffling the exhaust so it could scarcely be heard. The seat post tube was used to convey the exhaust from the cylinder to the muffler, the exhaust passing into the tube from the cylinder through the fitting by which the upper part of the motor was connected to the frame. This saved the use of a separate exhaust pipe, which would have been in the way.

On the top tube, just above the spark coil, were the handles by which the machine was operated. The handle on the right side was connected to the ignition timing device, and by raising and lowering it the ignition could be varied to take place at any point from the beginning to ¾ stroke, and with the gas full on, this would vary the speed from the fastest clip down to 3 or 4 miles an hour. The handle on the left side operated a valve in the gas pipe between the carburetor and the motor, and with this the speed could be varied to either extreme, or the motor entirely shut off. The grip on the right-hand side of the handle bar operated a switch by which the motor could be instantly shut off simply by turning 1¹/₁₆ of an inch.

To start the machine, the handles, gas, and ignition were placed in mid-position, and then the rider mounted as he would an ordinary bicycle. After regaining his balance, he turned the switch grip, the motor took hold, and the feet came to rest on the supports, and he was away.

This motorcycle was the result of long experimentation and much hard work. At first the

motor was hung over the front wheel and fastened to the fork sides, but with the extra weight placed so high, and since it had to be turned every time with the handlebar, it made the machine very hard to steer, especially going slow in a bad place, or among teams in a crowded street. Next the motor was tried behind the rear wheel on a line with the hub, but it was impossible to fasten it securely without adding almost as much tubing as was necessary in the main frame. At this point a machine was examined that had the motor placed in the space occupied by the crank hanger of ordinary cycles, and without pedals. This machine, when once started, and when running between 10 and 30 miles an hour, worked to perfection. Its only drawback was to get it started, even on the level, as the rider had to make a run with it and then mount, and at the same time be starting the motor. If the motor missed either of the first two or three explosions it would stop, and the operation would have to be repeated sometimes six or seven times before the machine could be gotten under way. It was impossible to start going up a hill.

After examining this machine, Marsh decided that the only place for the motor was in the angle of the frame just over the crank hanger, in which it would have a solid foundation comparatively low down and high under the rider. It was then necessary to make the motor narrow enough to go in this space without sacrificing its wearing surface.

Marsh succeeded in making a motor that, taking the initial pressure of the explosion to be as high as 600 pounds, had bearings of the same proportions as the best marine practice in steam engines, and was the right width. After this motor had been run for over 1,000 miles it was taken apart and checked, and not the slightest sign of wear could be found. It was believed that the motor would last from eight to ten years with ordinary use and reasonable care. The machine could carry any rider of average weight from 3 to 30 miles an hour and up ordinary hills without the use of the feet.

Around 1900, in Europe, where the motor-carriage industry was first developed, fully 70 percent of the self-propelled vehicles were of the three-wheeled type. Americans, too, saw the merits of the stability they offered. The E. R. Thomas Motor Company, of Buffalo, New York, made one that compared favorably with the best French cycles.

The gasoline reservoir and carburetor were com-

The Thomas Auto-tricycle (Scientific American, 7/6/01)

bined in a single triangularly shaped tank, mounted behind the seat post. The tank had a tube, the lower end of which carried a flat plate called the deflector, held above the level of the gasoline. Through this tube and under the plate the atmospheric air passed and evaporated the gasoline around the edges of the plate. The vapors passed through the throttle and air-mixer valves on top of the carburetor, near the seat-post tube, and were mixed with the proper quantity of air before entering the engine cylinder.

The crankcase of the engine contained two flywheels between which the crank turned. Besides its usual function, the crank pin also served to hold the two flywheels together, sufficient space being allowed for the free passage of the crank. The left-hand side of the crank case contained the exhaust-cam mechanism. Fastened to the end of the left flywheel axle was a pinion which meshed with a small spur gear, turned once for every two revolutions of the flywheel. Externally this gear was provided with a cam which acted upon a small shoe having a vertical stem whereby the exhaust poppet was lifted at the right moment.

The pinion performed still another function. Through its center a small shaft passed, terminating in a small cam whereby a spring was moved every second revolution, which spring in turn came into

contact with a platinum-pointed screw. The object of the vibrator thus made was to make and break the electric current so as to produce a spark in the combustion chamber of the engine. Current for the production of the spark was obtained from a four-cell dry battery incased beneath the upper reach-tube. The insulated wires extended from the positive and negative poles through holes in the battery box, twice around the frame. The circuit could be made and broken by a grip on the handlebar, by means of a key switch or safety switch at the front end of the tricycle, so that the machine could not be started by any one but the operator. The switch was operated by a small brass plug-key which could be carried in the pocket.

The motor was of the four-cycle type commonly in use. The speed of the tricycle could be controlled either by means of the gas throttle lever on the left hand side of the upper horizontal bar, or by the spark-controller lever placed somewhat in advance of the gas lever on the left-hand side. This second lever moved the vibrator so that the moment of contact was varied as desired. When the spark passed early the explosive mixture was ignited at the moment of greatest compression. A more powerful impulse of the piston meant more speed. When ignition occurred late, the piston had already started on its downstroke and the compression was not at its maximum, making a less powerful explosion. When the throttle alone was used to control the speed, the quantity of gas fed to the motor was limited, so the force of the explosion was reduced or increased at the rider's will.

The transmission gearing consisted of a small pinion on the end of the right-hand axle of the

A Motor Chair (Scientific American, 6/13/03)

flywheel, which pinion meshed with a larger spur gear inclosed in an oil-tight aluminum case. The spur gear was centrally secured to the differential gear. Like the transmission gearing, the differential gear was inclosed in a case. On the outside of the case was a brake pulley and a hand brake controlled from the handlebar by a lever. The brake mechanism was so powerful, the machine could be stopped within its own length.

The exhaust gases passed through a muffler placed beneath the rear cross tube, effectively lowering the noise.

Some of the machines that emerged were designed for elegance, especially a motor chair called a "morette," which was exhibited at the British Automobile Exhibition. It was built to carry one person at a speed of up to 12 miles an hour. A double morette, with a higher-powered motor, could carry two persons side by side.

The morette was started from the seat by a lever, had foot brake which acted simultaneously on the back wheel tires, and was steered by the tiller handle. The engine was located neatly within the front frame. The basket body was wide and comfortable, and strengthened throughout with iron stays. Elaborate precautions were taken to insure the comfort of the rider and protect him from any vibration from the engine or the road. The body of the carriage was isolated from the frame, cradled between luxuriant C springs, while a padding of vulcanized sheet rubber was inserted where the engine rested on the frame. There was also the vibration-absorbing quality of the tires, the well-known Swain tire being recommended as standard. On the single morette, tandem, nonslipping tires were fitted to the back wheels, and a plain motorcycle tire to the front wheel, the latter being also safeguarded within by the fitting of a self-sealing air chamber. In the double morette, motorcycle tires were fitted all round. The wheels were 26 inches back in back and 28 inches in front.

The morette engine was one of the most efficient on the market. It was automatic in every action, requiring no expert knowledge to manipulate it. It was a two-cylinder valveless motor. The flywheel carried on its inner side a rubber-covered driving pulley, which was in frictional contact with the tread of the front tire. The engine was carried on a bracket behind, and attached to the crown of the front fork. The engine was carefully balanced on both sides of the front wheel. It was lubricated on

the chop-feed principle, the oil being atomized as it was carried into the engine with the gasoline mixture.

The cylinder of the engine in action was inclined slightly upward. A carburetor of the latest type was fitted in place where the most even temperature was insured. The gas tank held a supply sufficient for 70 miles' actual use. The catalytic system of ignition was used where the electric spark was only required for the first explosion, the subsequent firing being automatic. Thus a small battery sufficed for an indefinite length of time, and unsightly wiring was entirely eliminated.

The starting lever operated through freewheel clutches on both rear wheels. At each pull the carriage was impelled forward a certain distance until ultimately the engine took up the running. The driving pulley, being in frictional contact with the front wheel, was rotated by this motion, and the engine started. A 1½-horsepower engine was used for the single carriage and 2½-horsepower for the double morette. This was sufficient for all general purposes, and would take the morette up the steepest hills in the country, always provided the passenger alit on these occasions, retaining control, of course, while walking, on the tiller handle. The object was not so much to provide a high-powered vehicle as one of moderate capabilities to insure comfort and safety.

The entire control was by the tiller handle, the grip of which actuated the current by rotation. By raising the handle the engine pulley was freed from driving contact, while by depressing it the engine could be slowed or stopped if desired. Thus the speed and the brake were controlled by one hand, while the double-action foot brakes on the back wheels were an additional emergency safeguard.

The morette was a distinct forward step in the provision of a practical motor carriage for the millions. With automatic carburetion and ignition, and instantaneous control of the engine and brakes by practically the same motion, the acme of simplicity was attained.

There were many devices employed to motorize bicycles, and one of the more striking novelties was a frame containing a bicycle motor and all its accessories. The inventor christened this product of his ingenuity, the "Motosacoche." Six wing nuts attached the device to any bicycle. In the illustration, the gasoline tank is lettered G, the spark coil S, the batteries B, the carburetor C, the oil tank O, the

The Motosacoche (Scientific American, *1/30/04*)

Motosacoche Attached to a Bicycle (Scientific American, *1/30/04*)

motor cylinder *A*, and the contact box *D*. A jockey pulley, *J*, kept the belt taut. The muffler, *M*, is mounted below the motor. The spark and throttle levers, *H*, were attached to the handlebar, and were connected with the motor by flexible cords. A twisted belt passed about a grooved pulley, clamped on the spokes of the rear wheel, served to transmit the movement of the motor shaft. In order to draw the air past the horizontal flanges on the motor cylinder, the motor was incased by two side covers, bulged in front to form a scoop. Not the least striking feature was its light weight, the motor weighing but 15½ pounds, and developing 1¼ horsepower. The carburetor, which used either gasoline or alcohol, weighed about 9 pounds. Two cells of storage battery supplied current for the ignition. The connecting wires were clamped against the lead terminal lugs instead of being fastened with brass binding screws, thereby avoiding oxidation and obviating the breaking of the lugs. The gasoline tank, with a capacity of 3 pints, held enough fuel for a journey of about 62 miles. Oil was forced into the crankcase by a hand pump contained in the oil tank. Sufficient oil was carried for a trip of 124 miles. The weight of the bicycle was increased but little by the addition of the Motosacoche, since the total weight of the whole mechanism was only 66 pounds. It was an efficient and lasting appliance.

12

Pioneer Tourist

A LITTLE-KNOWN STORY IS THAT OF THE SEC-ond man to cross the continent by motorcycle. A reporter, Frederick A. Talbot, interviewed the cylist, and the following story was printed in 1906:

Across America by Motor-Cycle

A FOUR-THOUSAND MILE RACE AGAINST TIME

During the latter months of 1906 a remarkable motor cycle journey, which was without parallel in the annals of the sport, and was a feat of physical endurance would be difficult to excel, was accomplished by Mr. W. C. Chadeayne, of Buffalo, who crossed the American Continent from the Atlantic to the Pacific Coast in the record time of forty-eight days. At first sight the journey of some four thousand odd miles does not appear to present many difficulties, but when it is remembered that the conditions for travelling in the States are totally different from those prevailing in England, the arduous and nerve-racking nature of the achievement can be somewhat realized. As one penetrates the interior of the vast American Continent settlements become more scattered, well-made roads give place to almost indistinguishable tracks, and these are

often so impassable that to make progress at all it is necessary to have recourse to the railway tracks, which, it may be remarked, are but little better, the uneven sleepers rendering it most difficult to make any headway, while the incessant bumping and vibration are not only highly injurious to the nervous system of the rider, but impose a supreme test upon the stability of such a light construction as a motor-cycle.

Then, again, the huge tracts of uninhabited country, where one may not see a fellow creature or the slightest sign of habitation for some five hundred miles or more, and the sense of utter loneliness experienced on these desolate wildernesses, are enough to deter the strongest-minded riders. The desert in turn gives way to towering mountain ranges, with their narrow paths strewn with huge boulders that have crumbled down the hill sides, over which it is necessary to pick one's way slowly and laboriously, while the numerous streams and torrents must be plunged through boldly, for bridges are quite unknown in these secluded parts. Such is a brief description of a few of the difficulties that must be faced by the man who is sufficiently intrepid to cross the American Continent in this way. The ride achieved by Mr. Chadeayne, as he described it to the writer, was full of hardships and privations, and abounded in thrilling incidents sufficient to satisfy the desire of the most enthusiastic seekers after adventure. Fortunately, this cyclist is possessed of a splendid physique, otherwise he would never have accomplished his self-imposed task. Here is the story as he told it to me.

I set out on this four-thousand-mile journey from the headquarters of the Motor-Cycling Club of New York on Thursday, September 13th, at a quarter-past nine in the morning. I had originally intended starting on the Monday previous, but was delayed by torrential rains of almost unprecedented fury, which raged for some three days, converting the country roads into veritable quagmires. However, at the first break in the weather I embarked on the journey, fully resolved to establish a record for the transcontinental trip that would be difficult to beat. I made no elaborate preparations for the journey, my machine being an ordinary 3-horsepower motor-cycle, such as is familiar in our streets, though it was rather highly geared.

I had not gone many miles before I realized the difficulties in store for me as the well-paved

Mr. W. C. Chadeayne as he appeared at the start of his four-thousand-mile ride (Wide World, 10/07)

thoroughfares of New York City were left behind. The unmade country roads were seas of mud and water from the heavy rains of the previous week. The machine slipped in all directions, and I was frequently brought to the ground. To add to my troubles, during the first day I had no fewer than thirteen punctures in as many hours—certainly an inauspicious start. To make matters worse, the rain came on again and fell with such fury that it almost blinded me. Still I plugged along doggedly all through the night, only stopping now and then to take a few mouthsful of food.

After leaving Buffalo for Erie I met good roads and thought at last that adverse Fortune was going to smile upon me, but as I approached Cleveland I quickly became disillusioned. The roads became a hundred times worse than those over which I had passed earlier in the journey, and by the time Cleveland was reached I was completely exhausted. Exposure to the inclement weather, together with irregular meals, had quickly told their tale, and I was carried off to hospital in a state of delirium. The doctors gravely impressed upon me that rest was most imperative, but after a few hours' delay, during which I somewhat recuperated, I mounted my machine once more, remarking that I was resolved "to reach San Francisco or bust."

Onwards to Chicago I made fairly good travelling, covering on the average about one hundred miles a day. On arrival in the Windy City I ran into the arms of a friend, who—observing my lamentable condition, for I was tired and worn out, soaked and mud-stained from head to foot—promptly hauled me off to bed and kept me there for twenty-four hours, meanwhile attending to my indisposition, which had developed. The rest was judicious, for, although I had already encountered numerous difficulties on the road over the thousand odd miles up to this point, my real troubles were still ahead, so that the loss of a day, although bitterly mourned by me at the time, proved subsequently to be a blessing in disguise.

From Chicago I made practically a bee-line to San Francisco, the route lying through Omaha, Ogden, and Sacramento. The country through Illinois and Iowa is practically an undulating plain for some seven hundred miles, but the roads are a negligible quantity. Normally they are tracks defined by the passage of cattle and wagons in the sand, but the rains had either washed them out of existence or converted them into treacherous swamps, into which the machine sank to a depth of eighteen inches or more, and the extrication of the cycle therefrom taxed my strength to the utmost.

More than once, owing to the wheels becoming clogged with the mud, which is of an unusually viscous nature, I was thrown to the ground, grovelling in the morass, and presenting a sorry spectacle when I at last regained my feet. Then the gradients at times were most appalling, and I had no alternative but to dismount and push the cycle to the top, sinking knee-deep in the stickiest mud that I have ever experienced. Yet despite these repeated obstacles and discouragements, combined with the fact that I was constantly losing my road, I contrived to travel some eighty miles per day. No halt was called at nightfall, but I simply plodded along as best I could, taking a bite of food when and where I could get it. For twenty-four hours on more than one occasion I rode along without tasting the slightest morsel of food or having a wink of sleep. At times I found the road so despairingly difficult that I took to the railway track. Progress was slightly better under these conditions, but collisions with unobserved obstacles strewn along the track more than once caused me to take impromptu flights through the air over the handlebars, though fortunately without inflicting any damage upon either the machine or my person beyond a few bruises.

When I gained Iowa City I felt so faint that a good meal and a short rest between the blankets, which I had denied myself for several nights past, became imperative. But this was easier said than done, for, covered as I was from head to foot in mud, and my clothes bearing sad evidence of their repeated contact with the ground, I resembled nobody so much as a tramp or hobo, who is the natural, detested enemy of the inhabitants in these Western regions. Consequently, in order to gain admittance to the hotel, I had to make terms with the proprietor, who considerately lent me a spare suit of clothes in which to appear at the dining table. This short rest acted like a powerful pick-me-up, and when I set off once more towards Omaha I was in high spirits. The cycle, like myself, had well stood the batterings of the journey, and it was only occasionally that I had to stop to tighten up nuts that had become loosened by the continual vibration.

Cycling across the great American prairies without a companion I found to be excessively depressing. I was completely isolated from the outer world. For hundreds of miles, on all sides, could be seen nothing but a rolling, uninhabited expanse. The telegraph posts lining the side of the railway, gaunt and grim against the sky in their monotonous regularity, were the only signs of the penetration of civilization to this inhospitable region. The ill-defined trail was bumpy and abounded with lurking ruts, and the closest vigilance had to be exercised to escape falls. Occa-

"I went on through the air." (Wide World, *10/07*)

Owing to his battered appearance on his arrival at Iowa City Mr. Chadeayne had to borrow the hotel proprietor's clothes in which to appear at the dining table. (Wide World, 10/07)

sionally, but very rarely, I passed a prairie schooner, the driver of which, with his wagon and team, roams over this vast trackless waste, and is the only human being likely to be encountered. Such meetings and greetings broke the tedium of the journey and served to spur me on, but I can assure you that it was with considerable relief that I struck a small township, and for a short while the dreariness of the solitary ride was broken.

Spills were so frequent that I became hardened to them. Before reaching Ogden, however, I had a serious fall, which, for the moment, I feared had brought the trip to a summary conclusion. I was flying down a hill at a merry pace, but at the bottom came into violent contact with a snow-bank, which the speed of the machine prevented me from clearing. The result was that the cycle buried itself in the bank while I went on through the air, pitching over an embankment thirty feet high. The concussion knocked me senseless, and I remained unconscious for over an hour. When I opened my eyes

I found by a fortunate stroke of circumstances that I had been picked up by a body of cowboys who happened to be in the district. My first inquiry was as to the condition of my machine. Though badly dazed by the fall I rapidly recovered. The cycle was only slightly damaged, the worst fault being that the wheels refused to revolve. However, a crowbar and a large wrench procured from a threshing-machine found near by soon served to repair the injury. Another day an amusing incident occurred. I descried an encampment, and riding up found myself among a nomadic tribe of Indians. They were as savage and as repulsive-looking an assembly as a solitary rider like myself could desire to encounter in those lonely regions. They could not understand a word of English, yet despite this disadvantage and their forbidding appearance they were quite friendly. They offered me every courtesy that could be conceived, but I was somewhat suspicious of their good intentions, as they examined my cycle too minutely and with covetous eyes. Fearing that they might suddenly feel disposed to dismember it among them for mementoes, I bade them farewell, and amid many vociferous "whoops," wishing me "God-speed," I left them.

In such lonely regions comfortable rest at night was out of the question, and I was consequently forced to make the most of the opportunities that presented themselves. My general course was to keep on riding until I became so tired that I could not keep my eyes open any longer, and riding accordingly became dangerous. I then sought the most advantageous place for a short nap.

In some instances the sleeping facilities were

A "Prairie Schooner" (Wide World, 10/07)

by no means inviting. One night, dead tired, I crawled into a disused and dismantled grain elevator, threw myself down upon the floor, and was soon in the arms of Morpheus. I had only been asleep for about an hour when I was roused by a loud scrambling around the apartment. I sat up hurriedly, and found the place swarmed with vicious-looking rats running helter-skelter in all directions. Sleep was now banished; I left the elevator with all possible haste, and was soon speeding along in the blackness of the night. On another occasion I came across a tumble-down shed, evidently used for sheltering animals. It was a rudely fashioned structure with a prairie-grass roof, and, although extremely draughty, the "hotel" afforded some protection from the night air and passable sleeping accommodation. Such luxuries, however, were very rarely encountered, and for the most part, when overcome by fatigue, I simply dismounted and went to sleep by the wayside, with my head pillowed on the cycle.

After leaving Ogden, where I was held up for three days by a blizzard, I passed through a series of exciting adventures, such as do not befall the average motor-cyclist. Instead of making my way round the north end of the Great Salt Lake I availed myself of the railway track, which has been built for something like forty miles on trestles across this inland sea. It was somewhat dangerous proceeding, as I soon discovered to my cost, for I had to keep a sharp look-out for trains, and had to cling tenaciously to the timber-work in a precarious position whenever a train passed, owing to the fact that the trestle is practically only wide enough to carry the train. By selecting this route, however, I cut off some fifty miles of the journey. When the opposite bank was finally reached in safety I struck off boldly across the terrible Nevada Desert. This is probably the most inhospitable and difficult stretch of country in the Northern American Continent. For some six hundred miles extends a waste of alkali sand covered with no vegetation beyond the sage-brush, which is prolific. The sun beats down mercilessly, and the ground reflects the heat, converting the atmosphere into a veritable oven. The fine dust penetrates everywhere, clogging the eyes, ears, nostrils, and mouth, and setting up the most violent irritation and thirst. The travelling is just like journeying over treacherous quicksands, the machine sinking into the soft sand until it can travel no farther and then having to be lifted bodily out.

To add to the dangers of cycling in the desert ruts and ravines extend in all directions, and, their presence being completely concealed by the prevalent sage-brush, falls were numerous. At places the soil was found smooth and hard, so that good headway could be maintained. When stretches of impassable loose sand were encountered I sought the easier railroad track. Travel-

A Tumble-down shed in which the rider passed a night (Wide World, *10/07*)

ling over this, however, was highly dangerous, for more than once I was nearly run down by trains.

On one occasion, when I suddenly discovered a train close behind me and prepared to dismount, the machine skidded and the front wheel struck the rail. Fortunately the collision threw the bicycle and me away from the track, and we were hurled some thirty feet down the embankment as the train roared by. It was a narrow shave, and great beads of perspiration stood out upon my forehead as I picked myself up, much bruised and shaken.

The accident had left its mark upon the machine, for the crank was badly bent. Repairing the damage as best I could with the available facilities, I climbed painfully into the saddle again and left the railway track for the dreary desert. The privations I experienced were intense. I ran out of food and water, and was famished with hunger and parched with thirst when I reached the first signs of civilization, having fasted for nearly thirty hours. Here I sought a few hours' sleep in the bar of an inn, the

"We were hurled down the embankment as the train roared by." (Wide World, *10/07*)

owner of which considerately placed this accommodation at my convenience.

Refreshed, yet suffering intense agony from the bruises I had received from the fall, I set off in the darkness, though fresh troubles were experienced at the start. The torrid heat of the desert had given way to intense cold, which froze the lubricating oil, and it was only by dint of great effort that I at last persuaded the engine to start. At five o'clock in the morning the motor gave out completely, after I had been on the road only a few hours. Completely fatigued, I resolved to await the approach of daylight before I sought the source of the trouble, and, despite the cold, I lay down and went to sleep on the railway embankment.

When I awoke I found that it was only a slight mishap that had brought the motor to a standstill, and it was quickly repaired. I still clung to the railway track, but it was hard going, for a long gradient had to be climbed. On reaching Reno my spirits revived, for I was practically on the border of California, and, although a difficult part of the trip still lay before me over the mountains, the end of the journey was within measurable distance.

Reno was left during the night, but I returned a few hours later, as owing to the inky darkness I did not see an open culvert, into which I pitched head-foremost with the machine, seriously bruising my hip and breaking a pedal of the cycle. At Reno I was lucky enough to secure a new pedal, and after repairing the damage set off once more. On leaving Truckee the road dropped slightly, and by riding all night I reached Sacramento at eight o'clock the following morning. This town is only ninety miles distant from San Francisco, but to my intense disgust I learned that by the road it was one hundred and fifty miles. However, there was no help for it, so I pushed on, my energies considerably revived by the fact that I was near my journey's end. In the afternoon, however, another accident occurred which delayed me for some time. I ran off a bridge and bent the forks of the cycle.

The night was well advanced when I at last reached Stockton and pulled up for a fresh supply of petrol. While the tank was being filled I fell sound asleep, and it was with the greatest difficulty that I was aroused. Half awake, I crawled into the saddle and sped away into the darkness, but had not been on the road very long when a deflated tyre demanded attention. At this point outraged Nature proved irresistible, and I fell asleep with the pump in my hand. Awaking at daylight I went on my way with redoubled energy, and within an hour or two reached Oakland, the journey practically finished, for across the bay I could see my goal—San Francisco. The ferry rapidly whirled me across the bay, and I entered the Western city at 9:10 in the morning on October 31st, having motor-cycled from New York City to the Golden Gate in forty-seven days twenty-three hours fifty-five minutes, and beaten the previous motor-cycle trip in the reverse direction by nearly four days.

When met by my friends I almost collapsed. For over a week I had not slept in a bed or taken my clothes off. As soon as possible I indulged in a Turkish bath and went to bed and slept for twenty hours on end. My face was tanned and weather-beaten, and the palms of my hands were horny and calloused from continual gripping of the handle-bars. Had I not been delayed a day at Chicago and snowed up at Ogden for three days I should have established a more remarkable record. My average speed throughout the journey was eighty miles per day, which, considering the difficulties I encountered, was not a bad performance. My best day's run was one hundred and fifty-seven miles.

I have come to the conclusion that record-breaking from coast to coast is not what it is cracked up to be. Any man who sets out to ride from New York to the Golden Gate for pleasure will not be disappointed, but when you have got to get there in a certain space of time it is more than likely that you won't enjoy yourself. It's all right when you've succeeded, but while you are accomplishing your aim things are vastly different.

13

Motorcycles of the Early 1900s

THE MOST PERPLEXING PROBLEM THE INVENTORS had in motorizing the bicycle was to place the motor in the most suitable position. In some cases the motor was mounted inside the frame, while in others it was carried on the front wheel, but neither system proved entirely satisfactory.

Then a motor-bicycle was invented by two Englishmen, Messrs. Perks and Birch, placing the motor in the rear wheel. By doing this the engine was placed in direct communication with the driving motion of the cycle. The engine was built stoutly and yet as light as possible, and developed a maximum energy of 2 horsepower. The total weight of the complete machine was only 110 pounds.

The cycle and motor contained many unique features and improvements. The back wheel was devoid of the usual spokes. The rim of the wheel was supported by two strong aluminum wheel flanges. Each wheel side was made in one piece, and these pieces when firmly bolted together formed a rigid structure. Within these two wheel sides the motor was placed, carried as it were on the hub of the back wheel.

The carburetor was of special construction, with a capacity of half a gallon of oil, sufficient for a run of about 50 miles. It was absolutely automatic in action. It was filled from the top in the usual

manner after removing the screw cap, and could be as completely filled as an ordinary bottle. Owing to the peculiarity of its construction, the engine continued to work at full power so long as any

Interior of Back Wheel, Showing Motor (Scientific American, 9/28/01)

113

petroleum remained. At the bottom of the carburetor was a small tap for emptying. There was no danger of the petroleum's escaping whether the machine was standing in a normal position or lying flat on its side, and there was no danger of fire from internal causes.

At the back of the carburetor was the atmospheric adjustment, consisting of a flat strip of metal on a pivot, which acted as an adjustable lever and could be made to cover one of two holes either entirely or partially. Its normal position was vertical and, except in decided changes of atmosphere, required but little alteration. When the exigencies demanded it, however, adjustment had to be made until strong and regular explosions were obtained by moving the lever so as to cover more or less the hole nearer to the side of the carburetor—the other hole needed never to be covered at all. In frosty, damp, or foggy weather it might be necessary to reduce the air supply, and occasionally to cover the hole completely. It was not necessary to alter the adjustment during the course of a journey after it had once been set. The ignition apparatus, like the carburetor, was automatic in its action. It was entirely self-contained within the wheel. There were no batteries, induction coils, or sparking plugs to trouble the rider. The current was generated by means of the small magneto-electric machine fixed to a bracket extending from the crankcase and driven by the revolution of the motor wheel itself. The current was conveyed from the terminal on the magneto machine to a point on the interrupter guide just below the ignition plug by means of a short insulated wire. Although the magneto machine itself could not be interfered with or detached, it could be bodily removed for cleaning purposes from the bracket to which it was fixed by detaching the nuts underneath. The vertical interrupting gear received its interruption motion from the revolving cam which actuated the small connecting rod, thereby giving the oscillating motion to the magneto lever, and also by means of the formation on its reverse side actuated the vertical interrupter and broke its contact within the valve chamber at the correct moment for ignition. If it was necessary to clear or to examine the interrupter gear at any time, it could be removed without taking the wheel to pieces. The main insulation comprised a good thickness of mica, which was highly effective. As the automatic parts were not liable to become deranged, very little attention was

A New Motorcycle (Scientific American, 9/28/01)

required. The possibilities of a short circuit were remote, but if one occurred, it was easily located.

The best feature of this motorcycle was the simplicity of the motor-controlling mechanism. Placed on the left side of the handlebar was a twisting handle connected with a lever, by which all the several movements of the engine were controlled. When mounting the cycle, the lever was brought up as close to the handle as possible. The machine was mounted in the conventional manner, and preliminary impetus was given to the velocipede by pedaling. When the machine was well under way, by turning the handle slowly the lever was depressed, which action gradually opened the supply valve and admitted the gas to the engine. When the lever reached the maximum depression the engine was working at full power, so any intermediate position produced any range of power and speed desired.

The machine was equipped with a powerful rim brake. To reduce speed the rider first raised the controlling lever and gradually applied the brake, which was actuated from the handlebar by a lever in the usual way. Care had to be taken not to apply the brake too suddenly or at any time when the engine was working at full power. The motor frames were built with low brackets, so when riding over a greasy road or through busy traffic the rider could put either foot to the ground without dismounting.

The vehicle was supplied with Dunlop tires of the motor type, so any danger of puncture was remote. In a test the cycle was ridden from Coventry to London and back, a distance of 176 miles, in 18 hours, including stoppages, though the actual time spent traveling was only 12 hours. An average actual traveling speed of about 14½ miles per hour was maintained throughout the journey. Stoppages were made only on one or two occasions for lubricating the mechanism of the cycle.

At the annual bicycle show at Madison Square Garden in 1901 it appeared that the bicycle had unquestionably reached its final type, with a marked improvement in the details and finish of the machines. The coaster brake had proved its reliability and convenience and was to be found on most of the models presented. Comfort of the rider was enhanced by the cushion frame as opposed to the rigid frame. The most noticeable departure of the year was the extension handlebar, which owed its existence to the tendency to narrow the wheel base of the the bicycle. This shortening of the wheel base brought the seat so near to the head of the machine that it was necessary to carry the handlebars on an extension in order to clear the knees of the rider. The change was introduced by the riders in paced races, but it would not be of much use among the average road riders, so the vast majority of roadster machines still had the old wheelbase of 44 inches.

A motor cycle was exhibited that carried the motor on the front forks and had a driving front wheel. It was another experimental model that failed.

Despite the many innovations, soon the consensus would locate the motor between the wheels in the middle of the cycle, where it would stay.

The motor bicycle supplied the "missing link" between the bicycle and the automobile, between the poor and the rich of the speeding sport. It made its owner feel he was still a wheelman in spite of the snorting motor on his wheel, and when automobiles of much larger horsepower tried to pass him in vain

Motorcycle with Motor Carried on Front Forks & Drive (Scientific American, *1/26/01*)

on the road, he was pleasantly reminded that he could hold his own among the swift company of the automobiles. The motor bicycle was far cheaper to operate than the smallest launch, it was much less liable to get out of order than the most reliable type of horseless vehicle, and it was the swiftest and most economic vehicle known in proportion to weight, carrying capacity, and fuel consumption.

A motor bicycle weighing only 60 pounds, of 1½ horsepower, could easily and safely carry a man weighing 180 pounds across the average kind of country road at a maintained speed of from 20 to 25 miles an hour. The automobile had not been built that would come anywhere near this performance. When it was considered that the motorcycle could carry three times its own weight and over, propelling this load at great speed and by virtually small horsepower, the amount of practical science involved in the building could be greatly appreciated.

There were some special developments along the way. The English Singer tricycle led the way, although it was ridiculed as a toy of very little practical use. Wheelmen jeered at the idea of comprising the motive power within the front steering wheel, but it was soon found that this unsightly but reliable machine could carry its passenger over British roads at a 20-mile-per-hour clip with no material drawback except the liability of the steering wheel to be jerked from side to side on rough pieces of road.

The English Derby motor bicycle transmitted power directly to the rear-wheel tire by means of a spur-gear contact arrangement.

Among other interesting foreign types was the Werner, which had a belt-driven motor attached on the steering head and outside the frame; the Minerva, of practically the same construction, with a belt-driven motor on the bottom frame tube flush with the crank hanger; and the Rex, chiefly remarkable for an aluminum bed fixed on the bottom frame tube, to which the motor was bolted.

A French motor tandem for pacing is shown with combination gasoline tank and wind shields.

None of these, however, was so good as the superior 1902 models of leading American makes. Both chain- and belt-driven motorcycles were popular, preference being shown for the belt driver. A round rawhide belt gave a smooth and much less jerky pull than a chain, was considerably cheaper, not quite so liable to break, and permitted instant adjustability. With a belt drive it was an

A French Motor Tandem with a Combination Gasoline Tank and Wind Shields (Scientific American)

easy matter to change motor pulleys from 4 inches for hard road work, to a 5-inch or 7-inch size when the roads were fine, or for speeding on the track.

Although the several patterns of American chain-driven motor cycles differed in model and in various constructive details, they were all of the frame-contained motor-chain driver, with the motor invariably placed within, and never without, the frame.

The Stearns, a 1902 racing model, was chain-driven. The odd-looking machine was designed especially for speed to replace the motor tandem in furnishing pace to the racing men. The rear wheel was very wide, the hub measuring 11 inches in width. This arrangement shielded the rider following the machine against any undue wind pres-

The Stearns Racer (3¾ horsepower) (Scientific American, *12/21/01*)

sure. In order to get the saddle down as low as possible, to further screen the rider, it was clamped directly to the upper frame tubing. The operator sat directly over the rear wheel, in easy reach of the motor, managing the steering by means of a brace of huge, elongated handlebars. The absence of pedals on this machine was explained by the fact they were entirely superfluous for racing. The operator did not in any way aid the progress of his machine. There were two foot rests or stirrups into which he was supposed to put his feet. A de Dion 3¾ horsepower motor furnished ample power to send this machine around the track at more than 50 miles an hour. The motor was of the high-speed pattern, making from 600 to 2,000 revolutions a minute, and the gear was 132 inches. The weight of the machine was 165 pounds.

Lighter models, such as the Patee Motor Bicycle weighing only 60 pounds, of 1½ horsepower, were being made. These could easily carry a man weighing 180 pounds across the average kind of country road at a maintained speed of from 20 to 25 miles an hour. The fact that a motorcycle was able to carry three times its own weight and more, in addition to propelling the load at a rate of speed prohibited on most bridges, made it very attractive to the public.

Among belt-driven motor bicycles, the Mitchell was undoubtedly the most characteristically American model. In simplicity of design, ease of handling, and efficiency of power, it was decidedly superior to any foreign machine, and unexcelled by any domestic make. The motor had a 3-by-3-inch cylinder and made 1,800 revolutions per minute, with 3- to 3½-horsepower, sufficient to propel the machine at speeds varying from 5 to 35 miles an hour. The frame was made of heavy-gage seamless steel tubing, and being only 24 inches high, was very convenient. The hanger was dropped 2½ inches, and the wheel base was only 45 inches, making a very compact and strong design with no suggestion of clumsiness. In order to balance the load more perfectly and secure a long belt pull, the motor was placed within the frame head directly under the rider's control, which position precluded the possibility of "skidding"—a not uncommon feature with machines having low-mounted motors.

The fuel feed was extremely simple and easy to manipulate. It was of the "drip feed" system, which did away with the troublesome carbureting devices so common on foreign-built machines. Instead of

The Patee Motor Bicycle (1½ horsepower) (Scientific American, 12/21/01)

The Mitchell Motor Bicycle (2 horsepower) with Flexible Rawhide Belt (Scientific American, 12/21/01)

the ordinary surface carburetor, a feed pipe was led direct from the gasoline tank into a small vaporizer. The quantity of fuel administered was regulated by means of a small thumbscrew with a pointer on an index dial indicating the amount of gasoline fed to the vaporizer. The air inlet was fixed, the volume of air taken into the vaporizer being gaged by the working piston. Instead of the usual throttle valve between the carburetor and the engine, a drip feed of gasoline was introduced through the vaporizer into the engine by the suction stroke. There was no more direct and simple form of liquid-fuel feed. After filling the fuel tank with ordinary gasoline, and the lubricating tank with engine oil, the operation of the motor was effected by opening the valves of these respective tanks, besides the compression cock. After mounting, a few revolutions of the pedals, simultaneous with turning the left grip, which served as a switch, to the right, three or four

sharp explosions were sure to follow, whereupon the compression cock could be closed, and the motor would now carry the machine along at a slow, steady pace. Speed was increased by moving the handle of the "sparker" forward; speed was decreased by moving the handle backward; to slow down temporarily the switch could be turned off, and to stop the machine altogether the current was shut off by turning the left grip toward the left and at the same time applying the coaster brake by pressure on the pedals. On coming to a stop the sparking plug was taken out, the gasoline and lubricating oil valves were turned off, and the compression cock was opened. These movements were simple, and after a little practice any wheelman would find himself in reassuring control of his machine.

Among the improvements in the 1902 model Mitchell was a ball-bearing idler, a speed device placed conveniently for manipulation, and a valve lifter. The mixer used in connection with the motor had the merit of not being affected by travel over rough roads, like ordinary carburetors. The machine was powerful enough for all traveling purposes. The efficiency of the motor enabled the operator to climb almost any hill, plow through sand, and go against head winds at a fair rate of speed, while on good roads a speed of 35 miles or more could be attained. Fully equipped for touring, with 1¾-inch five-ply tires, the machine weighed 100 pounds. The tank capacity of the reservoir was seven pints, which was ample fuel for a distance of 65 to 75 miles.

By 1903 even more improvements appeared in the new models. The Thomas "Auto-Bi" featured a number of important details. The cushion-spring fork absorbed all concussions and handlebar vibration, relieving strain on the mechanism and frame and eliminating all fear of broken forks, so dreaded in the past. The machine was driven by a 2½-horsepower motor through a peculiarly constructed belt. By an ingenious combination of leather and steel, this belt was made to have the unstretchable qualities of steel, while preserving all the elasticity of leather. This reduced strain on the motor and tires, and prevented skidding, at the same time it increased the speed of the motor and the hill-climbing capacity of the bicycle. The machine was provided with large flywheels. These, as well as the bearings and the connecting rods, were one-piece forgings. The bearings were all large, and were

The Thomas Motor Bicycle (Scientific American, 4/11/03)

hardened and ground. It was a machine built for strength, and yet the total weight was but 95 pounds.

The Metz motor bicycle had ingeniously arranged parts in the most compact manner. Tubing of a very large diameter was used for the purpose of resisting strains peculiar to motor-driven bicycles. At the same time the inner space of the frame was utilized for various purposes. The top frame tube served as a reservoir for lubricating oil, while the induction coil was neatly incased in the seat mast, where it was safe from injury. The lower tube served as a muffler, through which burnt gases passed from the cylinder. The motor crankcase was built integrally with the frame of the bicycle, and this, while reducing weight, added to the staunchness of the machine and prevented those numerous troubles attributable to a continual vibration of the motor. The flywheels were placed outside the crankcase, which allowed them to be of larger diameter than usual, and therefore of greater effect. The

driving sprocket was fastened to the crank shaft by a flexible connection. This flexibility could be adjusted to any desired degree of tension. The durability of the chain was increased, owing to its relief from violent impulses of the motor. Another important feature was to be found in the constant-level, float-feed carburetor. Three spray nozzles were provided at equidistant points around the mixing chamber which encircled the float chamber, so whether a machine was going up or down hill, a proper suction level was kept. There was also a trap for catching water and sediment in the gasoline.

The "Indian" motorcycle was another type of machine quite popular in the cycling world. Great care was used in the construction of the motor, and it was brought to a high level of efficiency. The problem of power transmission to the rear wheel was solved by using two chains, one of short length run from the motor to a countershaft mounted on a hanger bracket, the other transmitting power from the countershaft to the rear wheel. In the hanger was an eccentric for adjusting the chains. A speed reduction was made on each chain, and they were so constructed and arranged that it was impossible to break either one, even though the speed lever be thrown over to its full limit at the start. The entire power of the motor was communicated to the rear wheel, and a steady positive drive was obtained without any slip whatever. The "Indian" had one lever control, a feature important to the beginner and even to the experienced rider. In threading one's way through a crowded street, even the best of operators was liable to be confused by a multiplicity of levers. The single lever of this bicycle started and stopped the machine and increased its speed. The same lever lifted the exhaust valve,

The Metz Motor Bicycle (Scientific American, 4/ 11/03)

The "Indian" Motor Bicycle (Scientific American, 4/11/03)

permitting the machine to be started with but slight compression in the cylinder, and it also governed the time of the spark. The carburetor, constructed on the float and constant-level principle, embodied a number of new and important details. It allowed a steady flow of gasoline under all conditions of travel. The air was taken in through a hood at the bottom, and was adjusted by a regulator at the top. It was found that a better mixture was obtained by taking the hot air off the cylinder. The gas lever, which could be operated without taking the hands from the bars, was arranged to admit a larger flow of gas into the engine when extra speed or power was required. The machine had a narrow tread, which offered the advantage of a natural position when riding. Its total weight was only 98 pounds.

In contrast to this light machine, the heavy "Orient" motor bicycle weighed about 160 pounds. The makers worked on the principle that even the lightest of motorcycles was too heavy to pedal, and consequently the reduction of weight was not so important as a strong construction, which would prevent accidents and at the same time furnish sufficient power to drive the machine over the worst of roads by motor power alone. The weight of the machine also absorbed the vibration of the motor and prevented jarring of the machine and fatigue of the driver. A 3- or 4-horsepower motor was used for driving the machine. The best materials were used, since weight was not a limiting factor. Fluted copper rings were fitted over the cylinder to radiate the heat, instead of the cast flanges generally used. The accuracy and reliability of the carburetor had much to do with its success. The spark plug was provided with porcelain insula-

5-horsepower Twin-Cylinder Curtis Roadster (Scientific American, 2/20/04)

tion, which was found to be one of the best materials for this purpose. Power was transmitted to the rear wheel through a leather belt especially prepared and heavily stitched. This offered a flat plane surface, which was very reliable. The motor was thrown in or out of gear by means of a jockey pulley on a curved arm forming part of a handle.

In 1904 new models were still surfacing. The Curtis Roadster featured an air-cooled V-shaped motor of 5 horsepower, and was made by the G. H. Curtis Co., Hammondsport, New York. It was intended for use as a powerful roadster on all kinds of American roads. It weighed 165 pounds, and had gasoline and oil tanks of sufficient capacity for traveling 150 miles. The double-cylinder V-shaped motor was placed in a 23-inch frame, and transmitted its power directly to the rear wheel by means of a 2-inch flat belt made of two-ply Russian rawhide. A wooden pulley was used on the rear wheel, and a leather-covered pulley on the motor. The motor itself weighed but 60 pounds, had a 3-inch bore and stroke and developed 5 horsepower at 2000 r.p.m., thus making the bicycle one of the most powerful motorcycles ever built for use as a regular road machine. The crankshaft ran on roller bearings in hardened and ground-steel bushings. The two cylinders added greatly to the flexibility of the motor, and made it possible to obtain a wide variation in speed. With the regular gear of 4 to 1, the machine could climb any hill where the road was of fairly good surface, and could travel at the rate of 45 miles per hour on the level. With the racing gear of 2½ to 1, it made a mile in $59\frac{1}{5}$ seconds and 10 miles in $8:45\frac{2}{5}$ on the Ormond-Daytona beach.

The switch and spark advance were controlled by turning the left grip, while the exhaust valves could be raised by a small lever on the frame. The batteries and spark coils were placed across the

The "Orient" Motor Bicycle (Scientific American, 4/11/03)

upper part of the frame, the gasoline tank behind the seat. The carburetor was between the two cylinders of the motor. The company also built a single-cylinder, 120-pound, 2½-horsepower· machine. The two sizes of machines were respectively fitted with 2½- and 2-inch detachable tires, and had a 62- and 58-inch wheel base.

The new Columbia motor bicycle, built by the Pope Manufacturing Company of Hartford, Connecticut, had a chain drive through a speed-reducing countershaft to the rear wheel. The sprocket of the former, on which ran the chain from the motor, was fitted with two coiled springs, which transmitted the power, yet absorbed the shocks of the explosions. The motor had a 2¾-inch bore and a 3¼-inch stroke. High compression was used in it, and, at a speed of 2500 r.p.m., it would drive the bicycle 35 miles an hour. All Columbia machines were made to climb a 25 percent grade at a 15-mile-an-hour rate.

The batteries were in a case above the lower tube of the frame; the muffler was just below this tube; the spark coil was on the upright post; and the tank was over the rear wheel. The machine was controlled entirely by the lever of the plunger brake. Pushing this down speeded up the motor, and pulling it up slowed it down and applied the brake. The inlet valve stem and spring was exposed. Both inlet and exhaust valves could be readily removed.

Another model in the same year was a four-cylinder air-cooled motor bicycle shown here of 3½ horsepower. The bore and stroke were respectively 2.24 inches and 1.77 inches. Automatic inlet valves were used. Hitherto the four-cylinder motor had only been used in the construction of automobiles, but now their advantages were recognized. An explosion every half revolution insured a much more continuous series of power impulses than one every two revolutions, with the further important advantage that the use of the four-cylinder motor permitted a perfect balance between the various working parts being attained. Moreover, vibration was minimized, and the strains in the frame of the machine eliminated. The utilization of the four cylinders also allowed greater flexibility in the operation of the engine, the speed varying from 50 to 60 miles an hour. The motors were placed in a perfectly vertical position, which insured the best results as it was the only one that rendered regular and uniform lubrication, together with perfect control of the working parts. Furthermore, the motor

2¼-horsepower Columbia Motor Bicycle (Scientific American, 2/20/04)

was placed as near the ground as was feasible with safety.

The system of transmission was similar to that of the chainless bicycle. There were two bevel gears, one of which was on a longitudinal shaft driven by the motor, and the other was fixed on the rear-wheel hub. The whole arrangement was protected by a dustproof case filled with grease, to insure sufficient lubrication of the various parts.

To avoid shocks due to the explosions in the motor being transmitted to the bevel gears, an elastic coupling contained within the flywheel was interposed between them. The high-tension magneto was of a special type and had a current distributor of an entirely new type. The spark produced by this apparatus was superior to that attained by any other arrangement, and more easily controlled, the working parts being fully protected against mud, dust, or rain.

Although perfect regularity of movement was attained by the four-cylinder motor, smooth running of the machine was considerably affected by bad roads. In order to minimize this as much as possible, the bicycle was provided with a special elastic front fork. This embodied a combination of steel springs and some rubber plugs, and had for its object the avoiding of jerks. The fork was noiseless in its action, and conduced to the steady running of the motor.

The bicycle was also fitted with a new type of vaporizer, in which a special arrangement produced a perfect mixing of air and gas, thus insuring a complete homogeneity of the mixture. The automatic valve regulated the admission of the supplementary quantity of air at various speeds. There was also a new arrangement for lubricating the various parts of the motor, and distributing oil

Four-Cylinder Motor Bicycle with Magneto Ignition and Bevel Gear Drive (Scientific American, 1/28/05)

to the four cylinders in a uniform manner, while the machine was completed by a back-pedaling brake.

The design of the frame had been remodeled in order to embody the new features of this motorcycle. The inferior median part, which supported the motor, resembled a bridle, made of oval tubing, to which the case of the motor was fixed. At the rear end of the case an iron flywheel containing the elastic coupling was fixed on the motor. Above the motor, in the upper part of the frame, were two tanks, the forward one being for oil and the rear one for gasoline. To facilitate starting, a lever was placed on the handlebar, by means of which the exhaust valves in the cylinders could be raised to release compression. The motor could then be started by pedaling a few strokes.

The regulation of the speed was obtained by moving one or both of two levers placed above the gasoline tank, one of which varied the ignition, and the other limited the quantity of gas entering into each cylinder.

The machine had two brakes, one operated by back-pedaling. The ratchet wheel fixed on the bottom bracket actuated a rod which moved two jaws and thus exerted pressure upon a drum fixed on the rear-wheel hub. The other brake was composed of two long shoes acting upon the rear-wheel rim. This brake was operated by means of a lever placed on the handlebar and which, by the intermedium of rods, forced the shoes in contact with the rim of the wheel.

A 1904 invention was an entirely new arrange-ment for carrying a second person with a motor bicycle. A Thor motor was used, a sectional view of which is shown in the illustration. It and the attachment were made by the Aurora Automatic Machinery Co. of Aurora, Illinois. This sectional model of the motor shows the inlet and exhaust valves operating in their valve chamber, into which the spark plug projects. The crankcase has been cut away to show the flywheel revolving therein, besides the 2 to 1 gears and cam for operating the exhaust valve. The contact device is also shown on the side of the crankcase at the front. A curved spring attached to the contact box rubbed against a spring-pressed button, from which a wire ran to the spark coil. This curved spring acted as a switch, and in the position shown in the photograph, it made contact and completed the circuit to the batteries. When the contact box was moved back as far as it could travel by means of the rod connection running to a lever on the front fork, operated by a rack-and-pinion arrangement from the lever on the handlebar, the curved spring just mentioned moved away from its opposing contact and broke the ignition circuit. At the same time the top of the box struck a lever which raised the exhaust valve and held it open. This lever, and its withdrawing spring, can be seen in the illustration beside the curved spring and contact box. When the exhaust valve was raised, the current was automatically cut off. The carburetor drew its air from around the ribs of the motor through a small funnel at its base. The inlet valve projected through its housing, so that if

121

Sectional View of the Thor Motor as Used on a Bicycle (Scientific American, *1/28/05*)

the valve stuck it could readily be punched away from its seat by pressing the stem on the outside. The motor was oiled from an oil cup on its base, which in turn was fed from an oil tank above. The gasoline tank was arranged over the back wheel, while the forward member of the diamond frame carried the batteries in a case above it and the spark coil below. The motor was built in a diamond frame in such a way that it formed part of the upright post which screwed into its head. It drove the rear

Thor Motor Bicycle with Side Chair Attached (Scientific American, *1/28/05*)

wheel through a chain and an ingenious cushion sprocket having a diamond-shaped groove in which a brass ring of the same cross section was clamped between the driving and driven parts. This, and the method of confining the wiring to the motor, and thus dispensing with running the wires through the handlebar, were the main features of the Thor motor bicycle.

The bicycle attachment consisted of an extensible axle attached to the axle of the rear wheel and a curved tube extending from the end of this axle to the steering fork, where it was firmly attached. A wide seat was mounted upon this side carriage. It was so constructed that it could be quickly removed when not needed. The attachment formed one of the neatest solutions of the small automobile problem that had yet been made. The motor bicycle had ample power to draw it over not only ordinary, but also poor roads.

Inventors spent a lot of time devising lighter and more compact motors to be used in connection with bicycles. In 1906 a compact power outfit could be bought that converted an ordinary bicycle into a motor-driven machine. This unit could be readily attached by anyone with the aid of a few ordinary tools, as all the parts were clamped to the frame with bolts and nuts, and no brazing or soldering was required. By means of a chain, the motor drove a rubber-covered friction wheel placed in the rear triangle of the diamond frame, directly over the bicycle wheel. This friction wheel was carried in a fork pivoted upon the vertical post, and adapted to be pressed against the tire by means of the long lever shown in front of the seat. The machine was started with the friction wheel raised, and when the

A 2-Horsepower Motor with Friction Drive for Converting an Ordinary Bicycle into a Power-Driven Machine (Scientific American, *1/13/06*)

rider had it fully under way, he could throw in the friction, start the motor, and proceed under its power. In coasting or when riding in a crowded street, the motor could be stopped and the friction wheel raised. This was a very advantageous arrangement, as it was not necessary to run the motor except when it was in use. The whole outfit weighed but 45 pounds, and, with a 2-horsepower motor, the machine could carry its rider about 30 miles an hour.

Another power attachment for bicycles was invented in 1910 which called for no structural alterations to be made in the ordinary bicycle, and which could be attached or detached in a few minutes. The device comprised a small auxiliary wheel 20 inches in diameter fitted with a light motor which was connected to the rear wheel of the bicycle. An ingenious pivoting arrangement allowed the wheel a peculiar lateral and vertical movement, so that the steering of the machine was in no way affected and permitted the wheel to glide over obstacles or rough ground without transmitting any shock or vibration to the rider.

The motor was a small air-cooled, horizontal, 2-stroke engine with a specially designed hub to which the power was transmitted through a 6-to-1 reducing gear. The magneto ignition and vaporizer were mounted on the same plane, and in line with the engine, so that the whole was rendered very compact.

The engine was valveless, the inlet and exhaust being governed by ports, alternately covered and uncovered by the piston. It developed 1¾ horsepower.

To attach the motor wheel to the ordinary cycle, it was only necessary to remove the nut of the back-wheel spindle on the chain side of the machine, and to attach the frame of the auxiliary wheel to the spindle and bolt it up—an operation taking a few moments. A single-lever regulator controlling the motor was clipped to the handlebar, the connection with the motor mechanism being a flexible wire. This single lever controlled the action of the engine to a nicety.

The wheel complete weighed only 25 pounds, and the motor was capable of driving the bicycle at an average speed of 16 miles per hour on an ordinary road, with a maximum speed of about 18 miles on the level. The fuel tank in the mud guard was of sufficient capacity to carry the motor 100 miles.

Claude Johnson patented the "Max" motorcycle

A Power Attachment for Bicycles (Scientific American, 3/26/10)

in 1908. It was a light and comfortable machine of the "runabout" type, intended for short-distance work at moderate speed, absolute safety for the rider being assured. In the ordinary pattern no seat was provided, the rider adopting the standing position on footplates which were within a few inches of the ground. In this position the rider had perfect control over the machine. There was none of that feeling of fatigue and ennui generally experienced after a run on the ordinary type of motorcycle. This cycle would easily maintain a speed of 15 miles an hour (maximum). It would climb a hill of 1 in 6 grade at a velocity of 10 miles per hour. It was inexpensive both in the consumption of fuel and in maintenance. It occupied very little space, and the footplates folded up to form a stand for the machine when at rest. As the total weight was small, and the center of gravity low, it could be handled with minimum effort, and all tendency to side-slip was avoided.

The latest model was fitted with a special 1¾ horsepower engine with a back gear so a large belt pulley could be used. The frame was arranged with a continuous curved tube to carry the engine, these replacing the holding lugs used in former models. The wheels were 18 inches in diameter and were fitted with 18-by-2-inch tires. The fuel tank had a capacity of about 1⅛ gallons, or approximately

The "Max" Motorcycle (Scientific American, *12/26/08*)

ground, moved along over the latter just as an ordinary motor bicycle did. In its rotating motion around the circular frame the hoop was guided by a system of small wheels distributed and fixed in the periphery of the frame and bearing constantly against the internal surface of the hoop. The mechanical reaction necessary for starting and driving the vehicle was obtained from the weight of the frame, the motor and its parts, and the cyclist. The motor drove through a friction clutch, by means of a chain and sprocket, a gear wheel mounted on the frame, and this gear engaged with an internal gear fixed to the hoop. The friction clutch allowed of starting the motor independently of the hoop, and of transmitting motion to the latter by degrees and without shock.

The steering of the unicycle was very sensitive. In fact, in order to make it turn to one side the operator simply displaced the center of gravity by swaying his body. Despite this, and in order to make the control of the vehicle still easier, the inventor provided it with a small handwheel, the turning of which displaced the seat and rider to one side or the other. The brake was provided with an

enough for a 100-mile run. The control was effected almost entirely by means of a throttle and thumb switch, exhaust valve, lifter, front-rim brake and drum brake on the engine—all controlled from the handlebar. The weight of the machine complete was only 85 pounds. The wheel base was 39 inches, the length overall 58 inches, the total height 38 inches, while the handlebars were 18 inches wide.

Along with the practical, there were always the daredevils. In 1904 Signore Lilio Negroni invented a unicycle that was exhibited at Turin's automobile exposition and proved to be the greatest attraction. In the motor unicycle, the motor and the cyclist were mounted within a single wheel. The object of the inventor was to offer cyclists the marked advantages of convenience, safety, economy, and even aesthetics, over ordinary motorcycles. The unicycle consisted of a laminated steel hoop provided with a pneumatic tire and designed to revolve upon the ground. A circular frame was arranged concentrically within the hoop and carried the motor and the seat for the cyclist. The frame, motor, and cyclist together, when the hoop revolved upon the

A Unicycle Driven by a Gasoline Motor (Scientific American, *1904*)

automatic arrangement that prevented the motor and the cyclist's seat from becoming locked to the external hoop and thus being carried along by the latter in its rotary motion.

Signore Negroni did not conceal the fact that his apparatus was not yet free from defects, although these could be eliminated by appropriate modifications of each of the parts of the vehicle. He was convinced his invention would eventually possess all the advantages first mentioned, but it is not known if he ever succeeded.

Even farther out was the air-propelled motor bicycle invented by M. Ernest Archdeacon, well-known Paris experimenter with aeroplanes. He brought out a curious apparatus in the shape of a propeller-driven motorcycle in 1906. This he constructed in order to make experiments upon different forms of blades to show their efficiency. He claimed that the propeller, when well designed and adapted to the apparatus it was intended to propel, had an efficiency equal to other forms of mechanical transmission. To show what could be done in this direction, he built the machine, which was the first of its kind. What was more, it traveled at a surprising speed. With a small air-cooled motor revolving the propeller, the latter pulled the bicycle and its rider at a speed of nearly 50 miles an hour in an official trial over a stretch of good road not far from Paris.

On this curious machine a speed of 49½ miles an hour was made. (Scientific American, *10/6/06*)

Side View of Bicycle, Showing Arrangement of Motor and Propeller-Shaft (Scientific American, *10/6/06*)

In the middle of the frame was mounted a Buchet two-cylinder light air-cooled motor, with the cylinders mounted in V shape on an aluminum crank box. The motor would give 6 horsepower. It was located crosswise of the frame. On the shaft was a small pulley, from which a triangular-section belt passed above to a larger pulley. The latter was mounted directly upon the long shaft of the propeller, which ran in two ball bearings fixed to the frame and a third or outer bearing which was held to the frame by two long rods. On the end of the shaft was fixed the large aluminum propeller, which had perforated blades covered with gold beater's skin. A hand wheel was mounted at the back end of the propeller shaft to control the propeller for starting and stopping. A gasoline tank and spark coil completed the outfit, and the whole was very light, weighing not more than 150 pounds.

The practical use of this machine was to ascertain the comparative values of different propellers, so as to find the best form and adjust the blades at the proper angle, but sporting speedsters used it to attain new speeds in bicycling.

14

Off to the Races

THE SECOND ANNUAL RACE FOR THE INTERNA-
tional Cup, which was organized by the Motorcycle
Club of France, was held on June 25, 1905. This
was one of the best and most conclusive tests of
motorcycles which had ever been held in Europe.
As the roads were in good condition, there were no
exterior circumstances to alter the character of the
race, so the merits of the different motorcycles
could be seen. The machines gave remarkably fine
performances, in both speed and endurance.

The total distance was 150 miles, or five times
around an elliptical circuit passing through Dour-
dan, not far from Paris, each round counting 30
miles. In the different towns a certain distance was
deducted, and was not counted in the race. The
actual racing distance was five rounds of 29.2 miles,
or a total of 146 miles. Four nations were entered in
the contest. Each nation entered three of its best
racing machines, which had been carefully chosen
in previous trials. Their construction was somewhat
varied.

France had two Peugeots and one Griffon racer,
as shown in the picture (Demester the rider). The
Griffon was a record-winner and came out first in
the elimination race which was held previously to
the final trial, in order to select the champions. It

had a two-cylinder motor of V-shape, having 3.4-
inch bore and stroke. Accumulators and induction
coils were used for the ignition. A 1-inch belt
passed from the motor to the rear wheel. The frame
which carried the motor was not continuous but a
separate branch was fixed to each side of the motor
case and the branches were connected by a
crosspiece above the motor. The batteries, spark

*Demester Standing Beside His French Griffon
Racer (*Scientific American*, 8/19/05)*

126

Cissac on a Peugeot Racer. The Peugeot came in second. (Scientific American, 8/19/05)

coil, and gasoline tank, containing 2 gallons or more, were all placed above this crosspiece. A brake acted upon the rear hub and a second on the rear pulley.

The two Peugeot racers also had two cylinders placed at an angle. They had a 3.2-inch bore and 3.4 stroke. An induction coil was also used for the ignition. A Longuemare carburetor of a new pattern was used here, having a single float and two mixing chambers. This wheel had the lower part of the frame curved under the motor, so as to form a support for it and was thus made continuous. Two brakes acted on the back pulley, which was 16 inches in diameter. Two tanks were used, one for the gasoline, containing 2 gallons, and a second for oil.

England had three machines—the "Matchless," "Ariel," and "J.A.P." The Matchless was fitted with a twin-cylinder engine with automatic inlet valves having a 1½-inch diameter. The cylinder bore was 3 inches and the stroke 4 inches. The carburetor was of the float-feed type with rose pattern jet, made entirely of aluminum. The wheel rims were of the same metal and carried Dunlop tires. The frame and brakes were so constructed that by loosening the axle nuts, either wheel could be dropped clear of the frame to make repairs to the tires, etc. The contact breaker was placed on the motor case. An induction coil was used for the ignition. The machine was belt-driven by a Lincona belt ⅞ inch wide, with 6- and 16-inch pulleys.

The Ariel machine had a two-cylinder motor

which somewhat resembled the former, giving 6 horsepower. The cylinders were also mounted at an angle. It used an Ariel carburetor, and an induction coil without a vibrator furnished the jump spark. Above the crossbar was mounted a cylindrical tank and below it was the spark coil. It had a triangular belt passing from the motor pulley to the back wheel. The front part of the frame was braced by two additional supports.

The third English machine, the "J.A.P.," had a two-cylinder motor of 3-inch bore and 3.8-inch stroke, and it was claimed to give 6½ horsepower. It used a Watawata belt on pulleys which had a ratio of 1 to 2.8.

The German team used three "Progress" racers. These machines were all alike and had a low and elongated form. They were distinguished from the rest by the use of a single-cylinder motor, and also by the use of a megneto for the ignition. Their cylinders had a set of large cooling flanges. A Longuemare carburetor was used with this machine. The triangular belt ran between 6-inch and 12-inch pulleys.

Austria had three machines in the race. Two of them were of the Laurin-Klement make, and the third was of the Puch type. The somewhat peculiar shape of the Laurin-Klement can be seen in the photograph. The motor was supported by a curved

Wondrick, the Winner, with an Austrian Laurin-Klement machine (Scientific American, 8/19/05)

piece which passed underneath it. This piece was joined to the rear of frame by a horizontal bar. In the rear of the motor was the large gasoline tank, of square form, while the oil tank was separate and was placed at the top. The motor had a 3-inch bore and a 3.4-inch stroke. One peculiarity was the use of the magneto for the ignition, which was mounted in an inverted position underneath the motor. It was driven by chain from the motor shaft. The Puch racing motorcycle had also a two-cylinder motor with 3-inch bore and 3.2-inch stroke, using a magneto driven from the motor.

The Austrian, Wondrick, and Demester of the French team made the best time. Demester's machine undoubtedly made a higher speed, but the Austrian gained upon him in the long run. Besides, Demester had several accidents to his pneumatics, and even had to change a rear wheel, which eventually disqualified him for the race. Wondrick took the first place with an official time of 3 hours, 5 minutes, 15 seconds. A French Peugeot came in second. Wondrick's average speed was 61 miles an hour.

What was unquestionably the most powerful, as well as the fastest, motor bicycle of 1907 made its appearance at the races at Ormond Beach, but owing to the breaking of a universal joint and subsequent buckling of the frame, it made no official record. It was built by G. H. Curtiss, a well-known motor-bicycle maker, with the idea of breaking all records. The machine was fitted with an eight-cylinder air-cooled V motor of 36–40 horsepower. The motor was placed with the crankshaft running lengthwise of the bicycle and connected to the driving shaft through a double universal joint. A large bevel gear on this shaft meshed with a similar one on the rear wheel of the bicycle. The total weight of the complete machine was but 275 pounds, or 6.8 pounds per horsepower. In an unofficial mile test, timed by stopwatches from the start by several persons who watched through field

A 40-horsepower Racing Motor Bicycle Fitted with an 8-Cylinder V Motor (Scientific American, 2/9/07)

glasses a flag waved at the finish, Mr. Curtiss was said to have covered this distance in $26\frac{2}{5}$ seconds, which would be the rate of 136.3 miles an hour—a faster speed than had ever been made before by a man on any type of vehicle. Unfortunately, before this new mile record could be corroborated by an official test, the universal joint broke while the machine was going 90 miles an hour. It was brought to a stop without injury to its daring rider from the rapidly revolving driving shaft, which was thrashing about in a dangerous manner. Later on, the frame buckled, throwing the gears out of line, and the official test had to be abandoned.

15

The Motorcycle of 1912

THOSE WHO HAD WATCHED WITH INTEREST THE birth and development of the motorcycle, promising themselves the ownership of one when they became cheaper, more comfortable, cleaner, quieter, and easier to start and to operate, could find their standards attained to a high degree in the 1912 models. Greater advances were made in motorcycle construction in 1911 than in any twelve-month period before, and the price reduction arrived with startling suddenness. Practically every manufacturer had reduced his prices from $15 to $60 as compared to his 1911 models.

By far the most important improvement in the 1912 machines were that they had been made more comfortable. This was accomplished chiefly by the introduction of a floating or spring seat. The seat was suspended on a long spring plunger working in the rear diagonal frame tube, there being two springs, one for compression under load, the other for rebound. The arrangement was such that road shocks were almost entirely absorbed before reaching the seat, and consequently the rider was subjected to less shaking on rough roads. Still another method adopted to secure easier riding was the fitting of larger tires. The standard motorcycle tire was 28 x 2½ inches, but some of the new

models carried 2¾-inch tires as standard equipment, and nearly all were equipped with rims which would take that size.

No longer was it necessary to go through heartbreaking and undignified contortions to start a motorcycle. Just as the self-starter came with a rush on motorcars, the foot starter had arrived on the motorcycle. It was a pedal crank connected to the motor shaft by chain through a ratchet mechanism, and one stroke of the foot pedal "spun" the motor two revolutions. The starter could be operated with slight physical effort. It was simple and practically foolproof, and there was no danger of injury through "backfiring." With the foot starter the motorcycle could be started by a push of the foot with the operator in the saddle and both wheels on the ground, no wheel "jacking" or pedaling being necessary.

Perhaps the greatest objection raised against the motorcycle was that it was noisy. While much of this prejudice was unwarranted because the machines were quiet when shipped from the factory and were tampered with by owners who wanted more speed, the 1912 models were quieter than ever before. Mufflers were larger and more efficient, exhaust pipes also were larger and longer,

Foot Starter Coupled to Motor Shaft (Scientific American, *1/6/12*)

and the fitting of "tail pipes" for the final expansion of the burnt charge before its escape into the open air contributed greatly to silence. Muffler cutouts still were rather general, although there was no need for them with high-powered motors. It was the abuse of the cutout by opening it in cities and towns, either as a warning signal or "just because

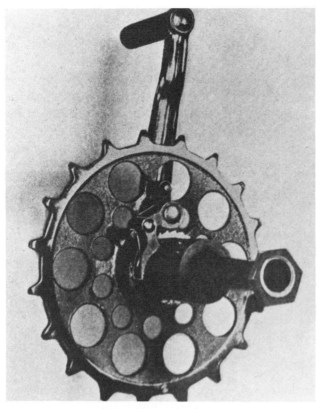

Ratchet Gear of the Foot Starter (Scientific American, *1/6/12*)

the rider liked the noise," that did so much to bring the motorcycle into disrepute with the public. Manufacturers continued to fit the cutout because they claimed that if they did not, many riders would remove the insides of mufflers or bore holes in them, and thus cause machines to be continually noisy.

Contrary to the general notion, it was not necessary to wear overalls and jumper on a motorcycle, and it was not impossible to wear good clothes and present a neat appearance, as riders would be better protected from mud and oil than ever before. Motors were made more oil-tight, and larger and better mud guards were fitted. The recommended attire was a light duster, puttees, cap, gloves and goggles.

In their pursuit of perfection motorcycle designers did not hesitate to borrow from their bigger brothers, the motorcar makers. They added such features as the multiple-jet carburetor, dry-plate multiple-disk clutch, and double brakes and roller bearings. The multiple-jet carburetor, as its name indicated, was two spray nozzles instead of one, as in the ordinary device. In the double-jet carburetor the regular nozzle was supplemented by a small one which had smaller gasoline and air passages, and gave a much reduced charge for slow running in traffic. For all ordinary running the motor was fed by the small jet, which always was open to the motor, and when more power was required, the throttle was opened, bringing main jet into action, and both jets then worked automatically in unison. When the throttle was closed the main jet was cut off from the motor entirely, but the small jet never was throttled. In addition to the greater flexibility, increased economy and silence were obtained with the use of the multiple-jet carburetor. The disk clutch also came into more general use. While it was made in several forms, the underlying principle of steel disks running metal to metal, or with antifriction lining interposed between the plates, was the same. Some makers placed it on the motor shaft, others on a countershaft between the motor and rear wheel, and still others on the rear hub.

Manufacturers began to use the double-brake system which many riders preferred with the big motors then in use. In Great Britain two brakes were required by law, but not in this country. The bicycle coaster brake in enlarged form was generally used. The automobile type of band brake of the contracting type also was very popular, and in the

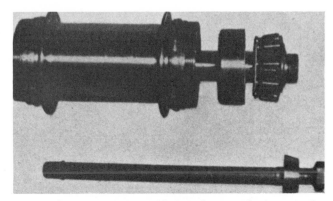

Automobile Bearings and Knockout Axle (Scientific American, *1/6/12*)

Wheel Equipped with Double Brakes (Scientific American, *1/6/12*)

double system was supplemented by an internal brake. Brake control was by foot pedal except in one instance where the double system was used, a hand control being fitted for the hand brake.

Magneto ignition was almost universal, although a few makers still offered battery and coil on their cheapest model. Improvements in magnetos rendered them better protected against short circuiting by mud and water. One of the bicycle makers who had entered the motorcycle field used a shaft and bevel gear drive for his magneto, as did a motor manufacturer, but all others depended on enclosed spur-gear drive. Automobile-type roller bearings for hubs were fitted to two makes. This type bearing had greater load capacity and durability than the ball bearing. Fuel tanks were larger, holding from 2 to 3 gallons of gasoline, and ½ to 1½ gallons

of oil. From 50 to 90 miles on a gallon of gasoline could be expected, according to the size of the motor and carburetor adjustment. The average oil consumption was 650 miles to the gallon.

There had been much detailed refinement in motors, but little of a radical nature. Cylinder dimensions remained the same generally, although two or three makers had enlarged these units. A four-cylinder engine was used on one make of machine. Bearings had been increased in size, and one manufacturer had changed from ball to roller, but the majority used plain bronze. Mechanical inlet valves were the rule, although one or two stuck to the automatic or suction type. The overhead rocker-valve arrangement was gaining favor, particularly for inlet valves. Valve mechanism showed considerable improvement.

In lubrication there was little that was new. The most general system used was an adjustable slight gravity feed to the motor, but three makers were using a mechanical pump, and hand pumps were fairly numerous.

The belt drive with flat belt was the leader, but the chain gave indications of returning to the high favor it once enjoyed. Every manufacturer of note, even those who built chain- or shaft-driven machines, also offered a belt model. The V belt was used to a rather limited extent. In the hands of the average driver, the belt drive gave the best service with the least amount of care, and even when much abused, it was the quietest and smoothest form of drive. In wet weather or on high-powered machines, it was at a disadvantage, and the chain drive scored heavily. The shaft drive was used by a long-established maker and two or three newcomers.

There was a general tendency to standardize models by building only two sizes of motor with many parts interchangeable, as well as wheels, frames, and other units. The two-speed gear was used by more manufacturers. Motor-car practice was apparent with sliding gear, planetary, and individual clutch types of transmission being used. Steering was made safer by strengthening the front forks, frame heads, and handlebars, and fastening the last so that they could not be wrenched out of line with the front wheel.

In appearance and finish the average machine of 1912 was handsomer than its predecessors, as well as faster, more durable, and more reliable. More important to many, it was cheaper to buy.

16

The Motorcycle and the Farmer

WHEN THE POPULATION WAS LARGELY AGRARIAN, the farmer's needs and desires played an important part in the economy. A motorcycle was considered a luxury to the city man in 1912, but to many farmers it was both luxury and necessity. It was a fast way to get to town without having to put in three or four hours on the road behind the family plug. The motorcycle needed very little care and was inexpensive to operate. It was used by many for emergency trips for parts during harvesting. The farmer could make the trip to town on his motorcycle, get the needed part, and have the machine in running order in less than an hour, while if he had to hitch up the family horse and make the trip it would take half a day or more. A motorcycle was handy in case of emergency, and speed in getting a doctor or some medicine saved many a life.

Motorcycles equipped with luggage racks could carry a load of 800 or 900 pounds if the weight was distributed front and back. They were used to make butter deliveries in town, and took vegetables and other products to market. A chair arrangement could be used on the front of the motorcycle and a luggage carrier on the back so two persons could ride for pleasure or business.

There were some bad aspects to the use of motorcycles on the farm. Some were used to run the washing machine, churn, cream separator, and other farm machinery. A belt was attached from the rear wheel to a flywheel on the machine. This was using a motorcycle to great advantage, but it was somewhat hard on the machine. The engine was

It means a quick trip for groceries (Scientific American, 9/5/12)

A trip to town for a bolt takes little time (Scientific American, 9/5/12)

Taking the cream to the station is a small chore (Scientific American, 9/5/12)

made to be air-cooled, and this was not properly accomplished unless the machine was in motion. If the engine was run more than three minutes standing still, the piston usually began to stick. The guard had to be removed when belting it up, and on some machines this required considerable time. The machine had to be held steady or it would throw off the belt, and this was usually accomplished by means of a rope. If the belt came off, it could get mixed up with the wheel, causing considerable damage. A motorcycle engine would not do its best work unless it was running at about 1000 revolutions a minute, and this was almost too fast for the average piece of machinery, so some arrangement was needed to reduce the speed. A countershaft usually was used for this purpose.

It was not a paying proposition to use a valuable motorcycle engine to run machinery when a stationary engine could be obtained for a low price to do the same work, but of course some farmers did.

An inventor devised a means of using a motorcycle to drive power tools efficiently, of course. A mechanical genius in Gettysburg, Pennsylvania, rigged a device that made his machine a portable power plant that operated his grinding machine. He specialized in sharpening lawn mowers and could double his day's output with less labor by this method. The engine was kept cool by fans, one on each side of the machine, which kept a stream of cold air blowing on it while running. The machine often operated half a day at a time without overheating.

A sack of feed fits on behind (Scientific American, 9/5/12)

Motorcycle as a power plant in the amateur's shop (Scientific American, 4/23/14)

17

Flying Bicycles

IN ONE WAY OR ANOTHER, THE SPORTS OF THE day kept life interesting, even if somewhat mad. Perhaps it was merely a desire for publicity, perhaps an exuberant sense of humor, that prompted Peugeot Frères to offer two prizes for flights made with the aid of human muscular energy alone. In 1912 no one, least of all a bicycle manufacturer, could plead gross ignorance of the first principles of cycling and of aviation, but a first prize of 10,000 francs was offered for a machine which, propelled by human power alone, would cover a distance of 10 meters (32.8 feet) twice in opposite directions, and a second prize of 1,000 francs for a machine which would cover a distance of 1 meter (3.28 feet) at a height of 10 centimeters (about 4 inches).

Although neither prize could possibly be won (the machines had to run on level ground, and having covered the prescribed distance, were to turn immediately and fly back to the starting point), Paris evinced an extraordinary interest in this *Concours de l'Aviette*. One hundred and ninety-eight entries were received, but only twenty-three aspirants to aviation fame appeared on the scene at the appointed hour. In the expectation of seeing a very novel contest, no less than 2,500 people witnessed the futile attempts of most of the twenty-three. There was much hooting, whistling, jeering, and much mock encouragement.

The ignorance displayed by many of the designers of the machines entered was amazing. Even elementary principles were ignored. Most could not get up a speed of more than 15 miles per hour, so heavy were they. Wings had been mounted on bicycles, apparently with no conception of the relation of lifting effect to speed and area of supporting

An Aviette (Scientific American, *1912*)

Aviette (Scientific American, *1912*)

Aviette (Scientific American, *1912*)

Aviette (Scientific American, *1912*)

surface. Some of the machines were provided with elevating and vertical rudders, some had no guiding device of any kind, some were fitted with propellers, and some had no propellers at all.

Apparently none of the men who entered realized that a regular motor-driven flying machine must have a speed of at least 25 miles an hour before it could vault into the air. Riders who had made it knew how considerable was the wind resistance encountered even at that rather moderate speed. The dramatic performance of men who had ridden behind railway trains (intended primarily to minimize wind resistance) had evidently been without effect upon the general reading public. If a bicycle rider found it difficult to travel at high speed on the open road, how was it possible for a man on an "aviette" to acquire a preliminary speed great enough to launch him into the air, when at either side of the machine wings were to be found that had an area of 40 square feet and offered an enormous head-on resistance?

Obviously impossible as it was to rise from the ground even with a monoplane aviette, some of the contestants were foolish enough to attempt the feat with biplanes. The entire day was spent as contestants made effort after effort to get into the air, although no one succeeded in leaving the ground. Consolation silver medals were awarded to the sixteen men who trundled out their machines and had the courage of their convictions.

In 1914 another "fly-by-night" device attained a speed of 70 miles an hour. It was a propeller-driven unicycle, built in Saint Louis and tested there. It was driven by an air propeller, which was operated by means of a gasoline engine. The big single wheel had a diameter of 81 inches, and was of aluminum, with a solid rubber tire. The rider sat on a saddle within the big wheel, and the frame that supported him, as well as the motor, propeller, gasoline and oil tanks, etc., was suspended so that the wheel revolved about it, leaving the frame in the same upright position all the time. This was achieved by a system of fiber bearings in contact with the inner rim of the unicycle. Two rollers and a pair of skids were located at the sides of the big wheel, and their purpose was to keep it erect while at rest. When traveling, the device balanced like a hoop, and

A Unicycle driven by an aeroplane propeller (Scientific American, *11/21/14*)

Winged bicycles again appeared in large numbers, and much strenuous training took place among contestants for the best flight, carried out with no other motive power than that furnished by the pilot. On August 11 Poulain, the well-known French cyclist, made a hop of 12 meters at a height of 1 meter, his speed being 9 kilometers an hour on his aviette, as the French called these little machines

these lateral supports were lifted off the ground. No stranger sight could be imagined than this exaggerated hoop, bearing down the road at racing speed.

The idea of putting wings on bicycles to make them fly did not fade away, although during the war attention was given to more serious matters. After the armistice, with the return of sports in France, there was a decided revival of interest in motorless flying, and by this time more was known about aerodynamics.

This winged bicycle is reported to have "hopped" 12 meters. (Scientific American, *10/18/19*)

18

The Eternal Bicycle

THE BICYCLE HAS ENDURED, AS THE FIRST LOVE of a people can never really die. It was modified, laden with devices, and changed in many ways, but it was in our culture to stay.

Since the object was usually speed and more speed, in 1914 Étienne Bunau-Varilla devised a wind shield for bicyclists. It appeared to be very cumbrous, but with it the cyclist could easily better many indoor records previously set. The inventor was active in the development of streamline bodies in airships, automobiles and airplanes, so he applied the same principles to bicycles.

The wind shield was fish-shaped and consisted of a light frame covered with fabric. When the cyclist was bent over in racing position, he was completely housed within the shield. A celluloid window in the front enabled him to keep an eye on the track.

The shield was better than the many projecting surfaces that had to be urged through the atmosphere when a bicycle was forced along, with each surface stirring up the air and leaving eddies behind. With a properly shaped wind shield the air closed in behind the bicycle and the resistance was markedly reduced.

Other accessories were introduced for convenience' sake. A device for making a bicycle stand still when it was stopped on the road could be ap-

preciated, for it would come into use in numerous cases when the rider wished to stop without dismounting from his machine. The supporting device shown was of the most simple kind, and was at once brought into use by pressing on a lever. On the lower tube of the frame and next the rear wheel hub was clamped a bracket. This served to hold a light steel rod on either side of the machine, which formed the support. The rod was journaled in the bracket, but, being a bent shaft, its lower legs took

A wind shield for cyclists with the aid of which Berthet has beaten some indoor records. (Scientific American, *1/17/14*)

137

Interior of Bunau-Varilla's wind shield. Through the celluloid window in front the cyclist sees the track (Scientific American, 1/17/14)

the position shown in Figures 1 and 2, when it was turned in its bearing. In the first position the leg projected to one side as a prop, while in the second position it was folded up against the side of the wheel. All the movement was controlled in an easy manner by the use of a lever, as shown in Figure 3. On the handle rod was mounted the usual brake, seen on the left, and next to it was a lever somewhat differently mounted, so that by pressing the lever a wire was pulled in much the same way as for the brake. This wire worked in the customary flexible tube, and it went down along the frame to the bent upper end of the pivoted rod or leg. A double wire allowed the working of both legs at the same time. A spring on the collar or support kept the legs held

up in the inactive position. When the lever threw them upon the ground, a suitable clamp or lock device kept them there so that the hand pressure need not be further applied.

This would make stops on the road possible, to enjoy the view or even to take photographs, and for this latter use it would be most useful in allowing time exposures to be made, the bicycle serving as a tripod.

Fertile-minded oddballs will always be with us. Spectators at the six-day bicycle race in New York in 1919 were astonished one day at the appearance on the track of a rider peddling away on a machine whose wheels had apparently shrunk to the size of a small dinner plate. Vertically, however, the machine was not dwarfed, for the rider—and he was a tall man—sat or virtually stood upright, in strange contrast to the plodding six-day contestants. Despite the smallness of the wheels, the newcomer had no difficulty in holding his own with the racers who were grinding out the laps at a pace of about 20 miles per hour. Only at the turns did he have any trouble. The banks were too steep for the pace at which the machines were traveling. Even the full-sized bicycles exhibited a tendency to skid downhill, and the new machine slipped so badly that the rider was obliged to keep to the level part of the track, at the inside of the curve. Nevertheless, he circled around for a full mile close to the pack of contestants, who were unaware of the strangely distorted wheel that was trailing them.

The rider of this odd bicycle was C. H. Clark,

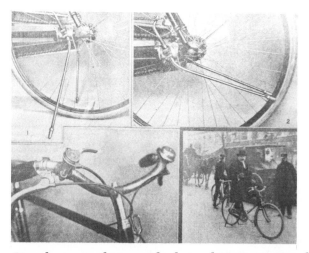

Bicycle props that may be brought into position by pressing a lever (Scientific American, 6/13/14)

Three ages of the bicycle—The latest type, the conventional bicycle and the old high wheel of the last generation (Scientific American, 12/27/19)

This bizarre bicycle has proved efficient for city use (Scientific American, *12/27/19*)

The easy-chair bicycle is obviously built for comfort and not for speed (Scientific American, *10/18/19*)

who invented the machine, not for racing purposes nor as a circus freak, but for real practical everyday service. It was a wheel that did not have to be left on the curb, but could be brought along by the rider, even in a crowded elevator, without taking too much space. It would run easily on paved streets and even on smooth country highways.

The search for comfort continued when a French mechanic designed a bicycle in 1919. While the conventional bicycle had been made in much the same manner for many years, motorcycle manufacturers did not take long to provide their cars with special backs for the seats, so as to reduce fatigue and increase comfort. So there came this bicycle which reminded one of an easy chair. It was provided with a steering wheel and horn, following French automobile practice, and was designed for solid comfort rather than speed.

For convenience, an ingenious Englishman solved the problem of baby-sitting when he and his

wife went cycling by patterning a side go-cart from a piece of sheet iron. An iron bar supported the body of the device from the fork over the wheel, and a shield was over the child's head. To prevent the baby from toppling over when the bicycle was at a standstill, an adjustable support that reached to the ground was used.

The search for additional power without the use of a motor went on. At an exposition held in Brussels, Belgium, in 1920, there was exhibited an extremely odd bicycle. While possessing the usual chain drive for the rear wheel, this bicycle also had

Improvised go-cart which is fastened to the rear part of the bicycle (Scientific American, *7/19/19*)

Rocking the handlebars up and down serves to drive the front wheel of this bicycle (Scientific American, 6/5/20)

Father, mother and baby on the road with their bicycles (Scientific American, 7/19/19)

a front-wheel drive in the form of a simple chain. The handlebars were arranged so as to be raised and lowered, and in so doing the power was transmitted by means of a chain to the sprocket on the front wheel. The upward stroke of the handlebars brought a pull to bear on the chain, which was attached to the frame at one end and to part of the handlebars at the other, and this pull gave power to the front wheel. The lowering of the handlebar caused the chain to return to its original position, freeing the sprocket wheel on the shaft of the front wheel. Thus every upward pull was a power stroke, while the downward push was an idle stroke. This double-wheel-drive bicycle was unexcelled in hill climbing, and the handlebars could be worked in conjunction with the usual pedals to the best advantage.

19

The Useful Motorcycle

THE MOTOR ADDED SPEED AND EVEN MORE convenience to the use of the bicycle, causing inventive minds to find many ways of aiding them in their work.

In 1910 London's Animals' Hospital rigged up an ambulance for conveying dogs to and fro. It resembled a Noah's ark in shape and was drawn by a 3-horsepower motorcycle, to which it was attached by means of an ingenious coupling device which prevented the ambulance overturning when traveling around corners. The ambulance was mounted on easy springs, was fitted with pneumatic tires, and was well padded inside in order to minimize vibration. Being motor drawn, it could do long journeys expeditiously, and ailing animals could be conveyed to the hospital and treated without delay.

In 1912 a Berliner brought out a motor bicycle that had the rider sitting in a comfortable seat and never in danger of upsetting. To a wide frame at the bottom there was attached at either side a small wheel which was normally off the ground when the machine was underway. When it came to rest, however, it tipped to one side and the small wheel held it upright. This was a great improvement, especially as there was never any danger of the machine's upsetting on slippery asphalt or a rutty road. The bicycle machine was fitted with a clutch and two-speed gear such as were being used on most up-to-date bicycles in this country at the time.

Small businesses who could not afford a standard motor truck and wanted something better than a horse and wagon, turned to the motorcycle with a truck attachment for light deliveries. The photo-

Motor ambulance for dogs (Scientific American, *1/22/10*)

141

Automobile bicycle with side wheels to prevent upsetting (Scientific American, *1/13/12*)

graph shows such a truck which could successfully combat a 6-inch snowfall at a speed of about 25 miles an hour. The vehicle was three-wheeled, driving through the single rear wheel. This made it unnecessary to use a differential, reduced weight, and did away with certain mechanical weaknesses. The vehicle shown was designed to carry 600 pounds in addition to the driver. The machine was started without raising the rear wheel from the ground, as was usually necessary in the standard type motorcycle of the day. The engine did not have to be cranked, but was started by the simple operation of stepping on a pedal. This enabled the driver to stop the engine whenever he left the truck

Motorcycle truck plowing through snow with a 600-pound load (Scientific American, *7/26/13*)

to make a delivery, thus saving gasoline, and also conforming to the law in certain localities, without at the same time being put to the inconvenience of cranking up his engine. The advantage of a motorcycle for light deliveries lay not only in the economy of first cost, but also in the fact that it used very little fuel per mile. The vehicle illustrated could make from 40 to 45 miles on a gallon of gasoline. It was estimated that the cost of operation covering 75 miles per day was about $16 per month, which was less than the average cost of boarding a horse, and a horse could not begin to cover a delivery route of this much territory every day of the week.

Many small businesses used motorcycles, including some of the thousands of students in colleges and universities who earned enough money by working at different tasks to defray part or all of their expenses. A student at the Kansas State Agricultural College who owned a motorcycle found he could make use of the machine in cooperation with the college dairy, doing a milk and creamery business. Besides delivering milk and cream to customers in town, he made runs into the country on his motorcycle, going out as far as 20 miles to purchase cream from the farmers and bring it back to the college. The milk and cream was carried in cans hung over the rear wheel of the motorcycle as shown.

In 1914 the average rate of speed on good roads for a motorcyclist was between 30 and 40 miles an

Collecting cream for the college dairy (Scientific American, *8/30/13*)

hour. Hence the rider, even in still air, had to face a wind so high as almost to assume the proportions of a gale. If there was also a head wind, the experience was like that of a hurricane. Even in the best of weather this was discomforting, but in winter the chilling effect could cause much suffering, and even frostbite. The inventors went to work on the problem and devised a motorcycle shield. It was merely a U-shaped frame clamped to the handlebars and the front fork of the machine. On this was stretched a canvas shield with a semicircular window at the top, although the shield was not so high that the rider couldn't look over it when he desired. How-

ever, in a normal riding position his eyes were on a level with the window. As an extra protection for the lower limbs, an apron was fastened to the frame of the motorcycle back of the front wheel, and extended below the foot rests. Thus the rider was completely protected by a windshield that added very little weight to the machine.

The sidecar made the motorcycle much more popular transportation for two people, but variations had to be made in snowy areas. With only a little snow on the ground, a motorcycle with its rubber tires had no difficulty, but when the fall measured several inches it was a different matter. A resident of Galt, Ontario, solved the problem in 1914 as shown in the photograph. The rubber tires were taken off the front wheel of the machine, and runners were bolted to the rims of the wheels. The rubber tire remained on the rear wheel of the machine for driving purposes, but the runner on the front wheel made the rut, thus permitting the use of one tire. The rig went through a foot of snow without any trouble at all.

There were many experiments in light-weight motor-driven vehicles ranging from the cyclecar to the motor wheel, but the smallest self-contained vehicle brought out was the "mon-auto" shown in the photo. It was a complete motorcycle and incorporated a number of ingenious arrangements. The wheels were 14 inches in diameter, and the 2⅝-by-3 four-cycle motor was rated at 2½ horsepower, which it was claimed was capable of driving the vehicle at a speed of 25 miles an hour. The frame was decidely simple, consisting only of a length of large-sized tubing, which acted as a tank as well as forming a very rigid frame. The total length of the machine was 48 inches, with a width of 9 inches and a height of 18 inches, just about that of an ordinary chair.

A most original feature of this midget machine was the simplicity of its control. The handlebars, besides doing the steering, had a swinging motion forward and back, and were so connected with the throttle and clutch that a backward movement of the handlebar closed the throttle, threw out the clutch and applied the brake, while a forward movement of the bar reversed these operations. Moreover, the further forward the bar was pushed, the faster the machine would run. These

A *windshield for the motorcycle* (Scientific American, *11/14/14*)

Motorcycle and side car mounted on runners (Scientific American, 3/28/14)

A handy runabout for war or peace (Scientific American, 9/18/15)

movements of the bar were instinctively made by the rider, so it was claimed that anyone could safely ride with no previous experience.

It weighed only 45 pounds, so could be picked up at will to cross streams, etc., or stored compactly in the house or anywhere.

Municipal services utilized the motorcycle. In 1915 a three-wheeled tired engine of light weight, low cost, and high efficiency was developed. It was good for a speed of 45 miles an hour, carrying two firemen and a complete chemical equipment, a reel of hose, a 12-foot ladder and all that was needed for subduing a blaze before it made too disastrous a start. It was a light scout car in the never-ending

warfare against fire that could also be used as an auxiliary to the heavier and more costly fire apparatus. It was also used in small, but scattered communities, which could not afford the larger engines. Its low cost, small size (making an expensive fire house unnecessary), and low upkeep charges adapted it particularly for a small village.

In the same year the Brooklyn Post Office tried an experiment in the handling of special-delivery mail. A letter or parcel bearing a special-delivery stamp traveled no faster than the rest of the mail, but on arriving at the post office station of its destination it must be delivered immediately. Where there were few letters to be delivered considerable expense was involved if they had to be taken out by the usual car. Since a lighter vehicle would do equally as well, in Brooklyn a test of motorcycle delivery was made. The machines were brought by the men and operated at their own expense. They were paid for their services at the rate of eight cents for each letter or parcel delivered.

The sidecar opened up many fields of usefulness for the motorcycle. One field was in cleanup, where a street-sweeping sidecar was attached to a motorcycle. In front of the sidecar was a steel brush which could be depressed so as to bring it into contact with the pavement. The brush then scraped and loosened the dirt so that the rotary broom which was immediately behind could sweep it up. A handle was fastened beside the driver's seat.

A motorcycle chemical engine (Scientific American, 2/20/15)

Motorcycle mail delivery (Scientific American, 3/27/15)

A motorcycle street sweeper (Scientific American, 7/24/15)

The motorcycle as an indoor tractor (Scientific American, 6/28/19)

When this was raised, the broom was lowered into contact with the pavement and caused to rotate. When the handle was lowered, the broom rotating mechanism was thrown out of operation. A machine of this type was particularly adapted for use on streets paved with asphalt or wood. One of these machines was tried out in Washington and proved very efficient.

During the war most efforts were bent toward arms production, but after the war the motorcycle found its way into all kinds of factory production. In a Hawaiian pineapple cannery it was used as a heavy hauling unit or baby tractor. The gearing was in the ratio of 26 to 1 in low gear, 16 to 1 in intermediate gear and 10½ to 1 in high gear. The hauling capacity was 4½ tons to a trainload of four cars each. It was figured that the pines were moved from the cooling floor to the warehouse, a distance of one-fifth of a mile, at the rate of 2½ cents a ton. Three machines were in use at the cannery, hauling from 10 to 18 cases of pineapples a day.

At times motorcycle engines were put to use outside the vehicles for which they were made. Vibration was generally a menace with most machinery, but occasionally it was deliberately created and used for odd purposes. Such was the case with the concrete tampers shown in the photo. It was an ingenious and labor-saving method of tamping newly poured concrete by means of vibration, with the motorcycle engine mounted on heavy rollers. The engine was deliberately unbalanced so that intense vibration was communicated to the rollers. The procedure in this case was to lay boards on the wet concrete and then wheel the device back

and forth over the boards. In this way the concrete was thoroughly and evenly tamped, in a minimum of time, and at minimum expense.

An ingenious little vehicle appeared on the streets of London in 1919 which was popularly called the "Tankateen." It was three-wheeled, taking its general design partly from the conventional motorcycle and partly from the small automobile. It had a 3-horsepower motor, which was ample to carry the load imposed by this miniature car. The Tankateen was inexpensive to buy and maintain, and yet it met the demands of those who preferred something less strenuous than the motorcycle.

At the London and Paris automobile shows that year it appeared that the trend of European automotive practice was largely toward the development of the heavier motorcycle. One exhibit was a

Using unbalanced motorcycle engines for tamping newly poured concrete is one of the latest tricks in modern road building. (Scientific American, 7/15/19)

Motorcycle with closed side car of Louis XV Model (Scientific American, 1/10/20)

Motorcycle built along automobile lines, weighing 400 Pounds (Scientific American, 1/10/20)

Another view of the new vehicle which is now meeting with much favor in England (Scientific American, 8/30/19)

closed-body side car of Louis XV model, which was a leading attraction at the Paris show.

Another unusual model was one that weighed 400 pounds and sold for 4,000 francs (about $800). It had regular automobile tires, big tool chest, three-speed gear, electric starting and lighting system, electric horn, foot rests, in a word, most of the features of the usual automobile.

The problem of comfortably carrying passengers occupied many an inventor's mind. A New York motorcyclist developed a miniature closed car, which made a rear apartment available for winter use. For light passenger service it could take the place of the hansom cab very nicely, as it had capacity for two persons and was very easy riding.

This vehicle was constructed upon a standard rear car and cost $600.00. The windows were of plate glass and access was had by two doors. The interior was made of ivory-tinted silk with an electric light let into the top. There was a small electric lantern on the hood above the driver's saddle, which bore the initials of the owner.

This type of conveyance had several advantages: it was small enough to be easily housed in a little shed, and its light weight made it inexpensive to run. Tire cost was small for the same reason. The inventor of this pocket-sized limousine predicted it would soon be a familiar sight on New York streets.

The English developed the convenient motor-

The miniature closed car which is readily attached to any motorcycle (Scientific American, *1/27/17*)

Front view, showing the motorcycle effect (Scientific American, *1/27/17*)

Motorcycle with special side car used in England for taxicab service (Scientific American, *6/14/19*)

The winner of the water-bicycle races (Scientific American, *9/11/20*)

A contestant with his combination marine screw and airplane propeller machine (Scientific American, 9/11/20)

cycle with sidecar into a public taxicab. By building a somewhat heavier and longer sidecar than usual, they arranged it for carrying two passengers, while the motorcycle carried the driver. The sidecar was provided with a top and side curtains, making it usable in all kinds of weather. The springs were properly designed and distributed so as to take care of road irregularities. All in all, the motorcycle taxicab covered any distance in better time than the automobile, and the fare was considerably cheaper.

When somber thoughts of war had receded into the past, sports and games returned to the foreground. Everyone was familiar with the speed and easygoing character of the canoe, and everyone had at some time or other come across the engine-driven canoe—generally a canoe equipped with a small gasoline engine of 1½ to 2 horsepower. Then Wm. H. Wray of Brooklyn came up with a modified form of canoe which he equipped with a 15-horsepower twin-cylinder motorcycle engine. This odd power boat was 16 feet long and carried three passengers. The engine drove the propeller by means of a chain, with a speed of 25 miles per hour easily maintained.

20

Innovations

IN 1912 THE TESTING OF STRESS ON MOTOR-cycles began in earnest. A manufacturer of motor-cycles in the Middle West had considerable difficulty in his early days with spring forks. He was using a high grade of steel, but still the forks broke in the hands of users. Consulting engineers gave the verdict that the spring forks were of the best that could possibly be made. One engineer, however, had made a change—not in design, but in material —substituting a steel somewhat more brittle. In order to prove to the manufacturer that he was right, he offered to test the motorcycle in the manner shown below. He rode a test track, banked at the turns, at a speed of 5 to 60 miles an hour, striking an obstruction (a 4 by 4 timber). Every time the motorcycle encountered the obstruction it leaped two feet in the air and alit 10 feet farther on. The test proved so popular it was adopted for general use.

By 1914 automobile manufacturers were using electrical systems to light and start their machines, so one motorcycle manufacturer followed suit by installing a complete electric lighting system even to the dynamo, and an electric engine starter as well, which was a giant step forward in the efficiency of this transportation.

Compactness in the electrical equipment was absolutely necessary, of course, and this brought about the development of a clever combined generator and starting motor that had a number of individual and highly interesting features. The combined unit was mounted just ahead of the engine, to which it was attached by means of bolts and

On striking the timber the motorcycle acquires a mounting position (Scientific American, 8/3/12)

149

Position of the machine two feet above the testing track on a ten-foot leap (Scientific American, 8/3/12)

Machine's position in alighting after striking the timber obstruction (Scientific American, 8/3/12)

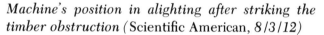

An electrically lighted and started motorcycle—the first of its kind (Scientific American, 2/7/14)

The mounting of the generator-motor unit (Scientific American, 2/7/14)

straps. It drove and was driven through a roller chain which gave a reduction of approximately 2 to 1. The battery had six cells and was split into two units, half being on either side of the frame at the back of the seat post. For operating the head lamp and the tail lamp the voltage was 6, but when used for starting purposes the cells were connected in series, giving 12 volts. To start the engine it was merely necessary to close a small switch on the handlebar. Immediately after the engine had picked up its own cycle of operations the switch was thrown the other way, making the necessary connections to charge the battery at 6 volts. The change in the mechanical unit from starting motor to generator was made automatically as the armature speed was increased. The machine was compound wound and with the batteries in fully charged condition delivered about 420 watts at 35 amperes for starting, the motor being sufficiently powerful to "crank" the gasoline engine at nearly 500 revolutions a minute. The time necessary to start the gasoline engine varied from about four seconds in warm weather to about 12 seconds in cold weather, provided the engine was in good condition.

The construction of the generator-motor was novel. The commutator was within the armature coils instead of being at the end of the armature shaft as was usual; thus great compactness was obtained. The four pole shoes were carried on the field piece casting and the brushes were mounted in holders on the case cover.

Field piece showing wind up—Casing showing brushes and holders (Scientific American, 2/7/14)

Armature showing internal—The controller switch arrangement of commutator (Scientific American)

Obviously, some device to maintain the output of the generator practically constant regardless of vehicle speed was essential and this was contained in a casing mounted just above the generator-motor unit. The device performed a dual service, for in addition to preventing the charging current from mounting too high at high engine speeds, it broke the connection automatically between the generator and the battery when the voltage of the former became less than that of the latter, as when the engine was stopped, for instance.

The battery was contained in two cases carried at the back of the seat post. The casings were substantial and the vents were so arranged that the electrolyte could not be spilled in the event of the machine's being turned on its side. The generator-motor unit was quite small, measuring 10 inches in diameter and 3½ inches in width.

Many devices tried on automobiles found their way onto motorcycles. The revolving-cylinder internal-combustion motor, which failed dismally when tried in an automobile, "proved" itself in connection with the airplane, and was tried in motorcycle service. A machine mounting a three-cylinder motor of that type was developed by a Connecticut inventor. The motorcycle pictured herewith did not differ widely, exclusive of the motor, from accepted practice. The motor was

mounted inside the rear wheel and concentric with it, so that the cylinder revolved in the same plane as the wheel. It was geared to the wheel by means of spur gearing, the ratio being 4 to 1. In common with airplane motors of the same type, the carburetor supplied the mixture directly to the base chamber through a hollow shaft, whence it was admitted to the proper cylinder through the inlet valve, which was positioned in the piston and operated by means of a cam placed on the upper end of the connecting rod. The exhaust valves were in the heads of the respective cylinders, being operated by means of a stationary cam, tappets and tappet rods in the usual manner. Silence was approxi-

Motorcycle fitted with a revolving cylinder motor (Scientific American, 4/18/14)

mated small holes before emerging from the valve pocket. Ignition was effected by means of a set of batteries and a single coil operating in conjunction with a high-tension distributor. While the maker claimed that with a motor of this type it was possible to lubricate all parts by mixing the requisite amount of oil with the fuel, as was commonly done with two-cycle motors, at first the system was not adopted, and the oil was fed to the crankcase by means of a sight feed drip, and was circulated to the various parts by means of centrifugal force. A free engine clutch of the cone type served to disconnect the engine from the wheel; it was operated by means of a lever on the handlebar.

The advantages claimed were manifold. Chief among them was light weight. The motor, which developed 9 horsepower when run at normal speed, weighed about 31 pounds, and it was claimed that the motorcycle complete weighed fully a third less than any twin then on the market. Another big feature was the total absence of vibration, for the three radiating cylinders were perfectly balanced and there were no reciprocating parts with relation to the frame of the machine; hence the motor was perfectly balanced. Also, the intervals between the firing of the cylinders being equal, another reason for smooth operation and reduced vibration was evident. By the same token, the torque was more nearly constant and the motor could be throttled down and run slower than even the best-regulated twin. Other features claimed were certainty of cooling, for the cylinders constantly cut the air, whether the motorcycle was moving or not, and the elimination of drive chains with their accompanying noise and dirt. The placing of the motor in such an out-of-the-way position opened the way for the adoption of an open-frame model for women riders.

The disadvantages were the inaccessibility of the vital parts, for the motor was closed in by the spokes; equal distribution of weight, with the greatest amount on the rear wheel, tending to cause skidding; the delicate parts mounted where vibration was greatest and where there was no springing, which was not conducive to longevity.

The daredevils progressed in their attempts at more speed, and in 1914 reached a new high. There were foot-propelled unicycles and motor-driven unicycles before, but now a unicycle was offered that was motor-driven and stabilized by a gyroscope. This would give the vehicle a stability it

Motor-driven unicycle stabilized by a gyroscope— The New York State barge canal (Scientific American, *12/12/14*)

hadn't had before. The idea was to build a large wheel with a track on its periphery and mount the car inside the wheel in a frame provided with three rollers adapted to run on the track. The motor was situated in the bottom of the car and drove the bottom roller by friction. The car tended ever to ride up the track inside the wheel, throwing the center of gravity of the wheel forward of its geometric center, and thus causing it to revolve. The gyroscope, in the bottom of the car, consisted of two wheels traveling in opposite directions. It maintained the wheel normally in vertical position. To make a turn, the car body was displaced laterally with respect to the frame in which it was mounted. This caused the wheel to lean, and hence to turn accordingly. In other unicycles the driver swayed his body to one side or the other to tilt the wheel. In this machine, as the gyroscope maintained the body in upright position, the movement of the driver had practically no effect upon the vehicle as a whole, but by operating the steering wheel, he could tip the big traction wheel to one side or the other. The gyroscope made side props unnecessary when the vehicle stopped.

Although the population was pretty much automobile-carried by 1916, many people still preferred the bicycle, although they wanted a light and convenient method of power to their mount to relieve them of some of the labor of travel. Many schemes were tried, and new ones surfaced regularly. At the motorcycle show at Madison Square Garden a new power plant was disclosed that appeared to meet the requirements of the bicyclist in a very satisfactory manner. The power plant was incorporated as a unit with the rear wheel. It was not an attachment to be placed on the ordinary wheel of the bicycle, but a specially built wheel, complete with all necessary mechanism that was substituted in a few minutes for the regular wheel. It was strongly built, with special rim and heavy spokes, thoroughly adapted to carry the weight of the motor, and to stand up under the application of power, which an ordinary bicycle wheel was unfitted for.

The engine was an unusually neat little four-cycle gasoline motor of 2 horsepower, which would drive the outfit as fast as was safe for a bicycle on ordinary roads, with an ample reserve of power for hills. To meet any question of balance, from the engine's being located on one side of the wheel, the main shaft of the engine was extended right through the hub of the wheel, and the flywheel was mounted on the right side of the rear wheel. This had the

Right side of motor wheel, showing flywheel (Scientific American, *12/23/16*)

Left side of wheel, showing engine and attachment (Scientific American, *12/23/16*)

Bicycle motor wheel attached to a bicycle (Scientific American, *12/23/16*)

153

additional advantage of permitting substantial and well-arranged bearings for the main shaft. An ingenious ignition magneto was built into the flywheel; and the drive to the road wheel was through spirial cut, nickel steel gears. There were two connections between the bicycle frame and the power unit. The rear fork ends were attached by bolts to a pair of collars that supported the power plant, which pivoted on these bolts. A pair of pressed-steel arms, which also supported the mud guards and gasoline tank, bridged the road wheel on each side and were attached to the collars of the power unit. At the forward end of this yoke was a curved rod that passed through a clamp fixed to the forward part of the rear forks of the bicycle frame, just behind the crank bracket; and threaded on this rod were two helical springs, one above and other below the clamp. This arrangement of yoke arms and springs permitted the power unit to rock on the pivots formed by the rear connecting bolts, which not only cushioned all shocks of the drive when starting, but also acted as a spring frame that softened the road shocks to the rider.

The control of the motor was through a single Bowden wire connecting with a small finger lever on the handlebar. The outfit weighed only 57 pounds, all of which was available for traction, and the half-gallon tank carried enough fuel for a trip of 50 miles. All moving parts were carefully protected from dirt and particular attention had been given to simplicity in removing the cylinder for cleaning, etc.

21

Cyclecars

IN 1913 IN ENGLAND, AND TO A LESSER DEGREE in France and Germany, automobile circles took a lively interest in the "cyclecar." These little vehicles were neither real automobiles in the usual sense of the word nor motorcycles. Americans, too, had developed cyclecars, or vehicles so closely akin to the typical cyclecar that they could be classed as such.

Undoubtedly it was the motorcycle that furnished the inspiration for the cyclecar. Most motorcycles would carry two persons, but hardly in comfort. At the time it was difficult to construct sidecars that would stand up and that looked well and afforded real protection to the second passenger; hence the cyclecar.

The typical foreign cyclecar was somewhat like a motorcycle, but they also resembled the full-fledged automobiles in everything but size. There were few restrictions on design, and yet it was necessary to eliminate parts that characterized the full-sized automobile.

Thus, the typical foreign cyclecar was minus the usual differential mechanism and live rear axle, and as a rule had no change gear set. Its motor was designed and built for the motorcycle, and adopted without alteration. As a rule, it was a twin-cylinder air-cooled motor. There were at least twenty-two foreign cyclecar models, and their transmission elements were like those of motorcycles. Seven of them were driven by means of belts to the rear wheel; of these seven, six had chain transmission from the engine to a countershaft; three were driven directly by chains and the remainder had shaft drive to either bevel or worm fearing on the rear axle.

In most, the steering gear consisted of nothing more complicated than a couple of steel cables running over a drum on the lower end of the

German type of the cyclecar (Scientific American, *10/4/13*)

155

A French cyclecar of the tandem type (Scientific American, *10/4/13*)

Cyclecar product of an American automobile manufacturer (Scientific American, *10/4/13*)

One of the newer American cyclecars (Scientific American, *10/4/13*)

steering column. The tread or wheel track was narrower than the standard 56 inches adhered to by the makers of large motor cars. The average weight was a little over 610 pounds.

American cyclecar manufacturers did some better, and the average cost of $500 was below the price of the foreign models. The American version was quite different from its foreign cousin. There were four cyclecars on the market in 1913, each having a change gear set, shaft drive, live rear axle and a differential mechanism much like an ordinary motor car. So while the foreign cyclecar was a thing apart, the American cyclecar was nothing less than a miniature edition of a full-sized automobile. The motor was four-cylindered and cooled by water. Three were block-cast machines with poppet valves, and one had a piston-valve motor. Each had shaft drive through a three-speed gearset to a differential-bevel-driven rear axle. The steering gear was the regulation worm and sector gear found on full-sized automobiles. The tread of two of the American cyclecars measured 37 and 44 inches, and the other two 56 inches, with an average wheel base of 94 inches. Average weight was about 800 pounds.

These small cars were the nearest approach to the true cyclecar made in America at the time. If they were considered as real cyclecars, they were easily superior to foreign models.

By 1916 everyone, rich or poor, felt he must possess a motor vehicle of some kind. The rich had a multitude of large and elegant vehicles to choose from, but the average citizen had less choice, although there were a number of moderate-priced

automobiles available. Even these were considered by many to cost too much to maintain.

It was to satisfy this market that the so-called cyclecars had been introduced, but the early specimens proved to be woefully deficient in many respects, and the price kept pace with the process of evolution, so the light car that resulted soon took its place, and became a comparative luxury, and out of the reach of the "great majority."

Another attempt to solve the problem of a vehicle for two was the motorcycle with a passenger attachment, first built as a trailer or forecar, neither of which satisfied the real demand, and finally a side car, which many found quite satisfactory. The combination of motorcycle and sidecar gradually increased in popularity, for its first cost was low, and it was both simple and economical to operate. But while it afforded comfortable accommodations for the passenger, the driver did not fare so well, as it provided him little protection from the elements and the flying dust of the wheels.

Therefore, another look was given to the cyclecar. An English designer came up with a model that would comfortably accommodate two people, give them practically all the comforts of a large automobile, and at the same time be low-priced and economical to maintain and easy to operate and care for.

It was odd-looking, but neat and convenient, and embodied a host of ingenious details. The chassis was built up entirely of steel tubes, combined to form a series of triangular structures in which the tubes were subjected only to tension and compression stresses. There were no brazed joints, but the eye-ended tubes were simply bolted together. If a tube was damaged in an accident, it could be immediately replaced by a telescopic tube, which was carried as a spare, and which could be adjusted to any position. For transportation the entire chassis could be taken down, and the separate parts tied up in a bundle. The motive power consisted of a two-cylinder, water-cooled, two-cycle engine, developing 5 horsepower, which gave a speed of 40 miles an hour on a level road; and as a three-speed gear was provided the car was capable of climbing any grade ordinarily met with. The engine was located on the right hand footboard, where it was perfectly accessible; and the entire unit, consisting of motor, magneto, and three-speed gear, could be readily detached when desired. The body afforded almost luxurious accommodations for two people, was provided with a wind screen and an excellent folding top, and the wheels were thoroughly mudguarded. The wheels were of the disk type, which were easily kept clean, and they were detachable. Each wheel, moreover, was independently sprung by a flexible helical tension spring.

The only thing lacking was a reverse gear, but as the wheel base was only 56 inches, and, owing to

Converting the motorcycle into an automobile (Scientific American, *11/11/16*)

Novel construction of the chassis (Scientific American, *10/4/13*)

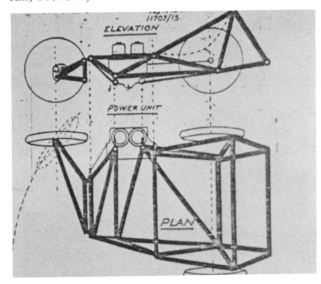

the three-wheel arrangement, the car could be turned in a 6-foot radius, the ability to reverse became of slight importance. It could run 50 miles on a gallon of fuel, and the tanks held a supply for 200 miles.

22

Women's Lib on Motorcycles

IN 1916 WOMEN WERE HOTLY ENGAGED IN their struggle for equality with men, but it would be four years before they were granted the right to vote in all states of the union. However, the war the world was then engaged in gave added impetus to the women's cause, since it was obvious that both sexes might be needed to defend the country. With this in mind, Augusta and Adeline Van Buren decided to make a cross-country run on motorcycles to prove the value of women as dispatch riders, and, incidentally, to help the female cause.

Their early training made them eminently fitted for the undertaking. At seven each of these girls was given a punching bag; at eight they were taught to spar. For many years they handled their own canoes in the Staten Island waters. Adeline Van Buren won recognition as a swimmer, Augusta was a prizewinner at skating. Both rode horses and were excellent divers, sprinters, and wrestlers.

The National Preparedness movement of the time was a hotly contested issue. As one newspaperman put it, "Aside from its value as a political issue, the Preparedness Program serves large numbers of people as an excellent excuse for staying away from home—particularly the women. Think of the opportunities it has given to the

women to display physical prowess in military training camps and various other fields of masculine superiority. Also to display their feminine contours in nifty khaki and leather uniforms."

Adeline and Augusta Van Buren

The Van Buren Sisters

The Van Buren sisters were twenty-two and twenty-four years of age at the time, and had been wearing "nifty" motorcycling uniforms for several years. They had driven their machines on local trips adding up to 9,000 miles the year before. To their critics, Augusta replied, "There is nothing dangerous about our trip and there is nothing to be surprised at. If people think it out of the way, it is the fault of their own point of view. It isn't that they are so easily shocked as that they think they ought to be. There is nothing phenomenal or unfeminine in girls being motorcyclists. Why should there be?"

A natural enough statement, when you consider the Van Burens' early training and the fact they were descendants of Martin Van Buren, one of our presidents. They were members of New York society, but with the blood of leaders in their veins.

On July 4, 1916, Augusta and Adeline Van Buren left the Sheepshead Bay track in Brooklyn on a trip that would cover 5,500 miles. They were mounted on specially designed solo Indian motorcycles, and would arrive some sixty days later in California with New York air still in three of the four tires. Their additional clothing was sent ahead to await their arrival, so they took only a minimal amount of luggage.

In a time when any man attempting a ride of this nature would go armed to the teeth, the Van Burens went unarmed. They asked no help, determined to make any necessary mechanical repairs themselves. The day of departure—Independence Day—was a fitting one.

They traveled the Lincoln Highway most of the way, via Buffalo to Chicago. When they left Chicago they were farther west on motorcycles than any woman had come before them. Augusta said, "Everyone has been extremely courteous to us and we have had no difficulties whatever, except the physical obstacles of the roads in muddy weather." She failed to mention fixing a flat tire on one of the machines. Also, the state of the roads in 1916 when it rained would be considered sheer catastrophe today.

From Chicago they continued through Omaha to Denver. Here they were told no woman had ever ventured up Pike's Peak at the wheel of any motor vehicle. So, with the daring that characterized their entire venture, they rode up the dangerous mountainside to the summit, adding to their achievements the distinction of being the first women to accomplish the unusual feat.

The weather report in the *Colorado Springs Gazette* for that day read, "Motorists going either north or south from Colorado Springs today will find the traveling heavy as a result of the recent showers which have made the highways muddy. The wear and tear of traffic over these wet roads has caused numerous chuck holes which will necessitate care in driving." Mountain roads could only have been worse.

From the Springs, the Van Burens went west by way of Leadville and Provo, using the Pike's Peak highway and Midland Trail. They were small in comparison with the man-sized machines they drove (Augusta weighed 107 pounds and could barely reach the ground with the tip of her toe when mounted on her motorcycle; Adeline weighed 117 pounds and was a little taller), but they were game for whatever difficulties they encountered. The rough roads, steep grades, and desert sands would have made the most seasoned veteran think twice before attempting the trip, but the Van Buren sisters were grimly determined to complete their journey.

Their resolution was put to a severe test in one instance when they were lost for seven hours in the desert sands of Nevada. With their canteens almost empty and the trail obliterated by windstorms, the girls rode around aimlessly, at times forced to drag their heavy machines through the pulling sands.

Late in the afternoon an old prospector in a tank wagon pointed their way out of the wastelands. They arrived at Fallon at dusk, worn out but not in the least deterred from their intention to reach San Francisco.

"Our transcontinental trip firmly establishes with us the fact that preparedness is the whole secret of success," Augusta said. "Our aim in making this long cross-country run was to point out for our own benefit and for that of the women of this country, that women can be of real efficient aid to our Nation in case of need, if they will only devote a little of their time toward urging and schooling for National Preparedness. Knowing that in making this trip we were bound to encounter all kinds of weather and road conditions, from the best to the worst, we gave careful thought to our preparation. We took particular care of our equipment and were ready for any emergency."

The Van Burens belonged to the National Security League in the capacity of dispatch bearers, ready for call in time of war. They wanted to establish women as motorcycle dispatch riders so that on their return to New York they could organize and train for the Special Aid Society of New York City, a group of women who would rival men as messengers. Adeline and Augusta spread defense propaganda all along their route, hoping to arouse more interest in the movement.

Friends, motorcycle dealers, and tire companies hosted the girls along the way, partially offsetting the experiences the ladies had with the law. The Van Burens were clad in leather caps, coats, breeches and leggings—a natural costume for motorcycle riding. However, their "men's clothing" got them arrested several times in small towns between Chicago and the Rockies, although

The Van Burens being welcomed by a representative of the movie companies in Hollywood

Sightseeing

they were never put in jail. In each case they were released with a reprimand, provided they left town at once.

Their newspaper publicity was disappointing. Small articles reported their progress, but with the usual condescension of that time. The *Colorado Springs Gazette*, on August 6, 1916, reported their mountain-climbing success, adding, "They are of the out-of-doors sort of young women by habit and quite frequently tour through their home state on their vacations. Each has two and a half months at her disposal this year and they determined to take one big trip and see America at first hand."

Their arrival in San Francisco was a great disappointment. The Van Burens reached the city at a bad time, for it was Labor Day weekend. They

160

expected to be met by a large delegation from the San Francisco Motorcycle Club, but nary a wheelman greeted them. Apparently, they were all gone for the holiday.

The reception was discouraging to the ladies, and they decided San Francisco was a "hick hamlet" indeed. The *Chronicle* gave them only three inches of column saying, "The young women mounted their cycles in New York City on July 4. They putt-putted along Lincoln Highway by easy stages, taking in all the side trips."

Augusta's report gave more detail. "That preparedness pays is demonstrated in the fact that we arrived in San Francisco without having encountered any serious trouble and with New York air still in our tires. We naturally take a little pride in our trip because we are the first women to have crossed the continent on motorcycles. The whole trip was a perilous one for two girls to undertake alone. It had its hazards, but it had its pleasures, too, and it all goes to prove that woman 'can if she will.' "

They proceeded south in California, deciding to complete their trip by seeing as much as they could. They visited points of interest along the way, and were welcomed in Hollywood by a representative of the movie companies. They made plans to motor to San Diego, then ship their machines back to New York and return home by train. "We would dearly love to drive back, but we must be at work by the first week in September," they said. Adeline was an English teacher in the New York City public school system, Augusta a correspondent in a business school. They had planned to spend a week on the coast, but time denied them their earned vacation.

On their arrival in New York, the girls returned to their respective jobs without fanfare. The ultimate put-down was the lead editorial in the Pacific Motorcyclist published two weeks later. It hailed not the maids, only their machines! "If young girls of normal physique can make such a journey without difficulty and without any outside assistance, what possible excuse can any *man* have for hesitating over any ride he may wish to take on his machine?"

The editorial went on to say the Van Burens had demonstrated the absolute reliability of American-built motorcycles. Also, "the fact that these girls made the greatest motor trip possible in this country without escort, and were never subjected to insult or indignity in their journey, proves conclusively that the alleged wild and woolly west now is but a memory, and that the vast country west of the Mississippi is as safe for unprotected women as the effete East."

23

War Wheels

WHEN WORLD WAR I ERUPTED, ENGLAND WAS undoubtedly the home of the two-wheeled motor carriage, although the invention belonged to France. All the warring nations had motorcycles, but there were undoubtedly many more German and French motorcycles in war service than English. At the outbreak of the conflict all the Continental nations concerned commandeered every motor vehicle of whatever type. In England, while there was no confiscation of power vehicles, large numbers of motorcycles were offered voluntarily to the government. Soon after war was declared there was a great meeting of motorcyclists at Wimbledon Common, who gathered together to offer their services to the army. Although the work of the motorcyclists was by no means as conspicuous as that of other branches of the service, there is no doubt that they proved invaluable to the respective colors they served. They did all the work that had once been done by the mounted courier, and much more besides. They carried messages between one end of a column and another, and it was a common sight to see a gas-masked cyclist speeding through a gas-soaked village. They acted as police on the roads behind the battle line. They served as guides for motor trucks and as scouts for automobile con-

voys, examining the roads to see that bridges were in good condition and that there were no impassable obstacles. They even did much of the reconnoitering formerly done by the cavalry alone. In all such work their enormous speed as compared with

British motorcyclists assembled at Wimbledon Common to offer their service to the army (Scientific American, 2/6/15)

162

Side car of American design carrying a Colt automatic (Scientific American, *2/6/15*)

Gas-masked courier (Scientific American, *2/6/15*)

French motorcycle scout and his canine assistant (Scientific American, *2/6/15*)

it. One motorcycle scout belonging to the French army in Belgium used his side car chiefly to carry a dog that accompanied him on all his expeditions. When he had an important message to send back to headquarters, but did not wish to interrupt his reconnoitering, he wrote the message on a slip of paper which was fastened to the dog's collar, sent the dog to headquarters, and proceeded on his way.

The side car made it possible to convert the motorcycle into a fighting machine. Several machines were used in the conflict that were equipped with automatic guns. The Americans had a motorcycle sidecar built especially for fighting purposes, on which a Colt automatic gun of rifle caliber was mounted. Provision was made for carrying two passengers, so that it was possible to operate the gun while the machine was in motion. This greatly increased its field of usefulness. The gun had a firing capacity of 450 or more shots per minute and, if desired, could be detached from the special mount on the machine and used on a portable tripod which was collapsible and carried on the sidecar. The machine was equipped with a 15-horsepower twin-cylinder motor and had a two-speed gear, the low speed permitting it to be used for cross-country work, if necessary. On the road it would run up to a speed of 40 miles per hour, and it had a radius of 75 miles on a tankful of gasoline.

London started its machine-gun battery with a Lewis gun that was operated from a sidecar. Other English armed motorcycles were provided with bullet-proof steel guards to protect the man in the sidecar and also vital parts of the driver of the machine. A shield was attached to the handlebar

that of a horse was of tremendous importance. The only drawback was that they could not run freely across country or over roads that were in very bad repair or obstructed by fallen trees or telegraph poles.

The side car was often used as a carrier for luggage and also for the purpose of transporting a fellow soldier or officer when conditions demanded

British side car fitted with a Lewis machine gun (Scientific American, 2/6/15)

and had a bullet-proof guard that extended well over the front wheel to protect the tire from puncture. In the early days of the war a battery of eighteen motor machine guns was sent across the Channel, six fitted with Maxim machine guns, six with spare gun carriages, and six to carry ammunition.

Even Canada was represented when Quartermaster-Sergeant H. R. Northover of the Nine-tieth Regiment of Canada Militia designed a fighting machine. The motorcycle with Maxim gun mounted on a sidecar chassis had a greatly increased radius of effective action as compared with other artillery. It could travel 4 miles per hour (the pace of infantry march) or be hurried to a distant point at a rate faster than 40 miles per hour.

When word was received that the Ninetieth Regiment probably would be in the first division from Canada to be sent to Europe, the motorcycle artillery was driven for 2½ hours through lines of people extending from the sidewalk to the middle of the road. It traveled through water and plowed fields, and went everywhere with the rest of the artillery. Its superior speed and the rapidity with which it could be mobilized where needed were the chief advantages.

War is a terrible business, and a certain callousness toward the customs of humanity is inevitable. If a man was ready to give his life for his country, it was assumed that he was equally willing to accept suffering, and the success of the armed forces was of paramount importance. Therefore, it was a harsh but true condition of battle that the first object of the medical service was not to relieve suffering, not to face danger through more humanitarian principles, but to further the operations of the army by seeing to it that the disabled were cleared away

A British cyclist machine gun battery (Scientific American, 2/6/15)

164

A Motorcycle machine gun (Scientific American, 2/6/15)

A Motorcycle ambulance for line-of-fire service (Scientific American, 8/5/16)

The double-decker motorcycle ambulance in actual service, showing arrangement of the wounded (Scientific American, 8/5/16)

Rear view of the double-decker motorcycle ambulance. Note first-aid cabinet mounted below the stretchers (Scientific American, 8/5/16)

from the front for the reason that if allowed to remain they might interfere with the achievement of victory. Motorcycle ambulances were deemed the most speedy and efficient vehicles to remove the injured from the field of battle.

Variations were made, one a double-decker device introduced by an American manufacturer, to accommodate two patients on each trip. Regulation stretchers were used, fitted with special pedestals set into sections of the carrier frames, where they were clamped to prevent slipping. The chassis on which was mounted the stretcher frame was of special reinforced construction with such features as vanadium steel springs and adjustable tread. The machine would climb the steepest hills and had a speed up to 60 miles per hour on the level. A cradle-spring frame, three speeds, a starter, double controls, and a heavy duty clutch were among the

special features which were said to make it most adaptable to hospital work.

A first-aid cabinet was mounted below the lower stretcher on the chassis of the motorcycle ambulance. This afforded opportunity for the ambulance attendants to give dressings right on the battlefield without the delay which would occur if the patient had to be moved to the hospital in the rear. These ambulances proved of extraordinary value in the European war theater.

The British Red Cross Society also had a motorcycle ambulance side car for service. The machine was of standard 8-horsepower type with

The side car ambulance hastening to the hospital (Scientific American, 8/5/16)

Placing the wounded in the motorcycle ambulance (Scientific American, 8/5/16)

semiautomatic lubrication and magneto ignition. The speed gear was of the three-speed countershaft type. The ambulance portion was of an entirely original design. It was constructed of tubular framework and so arranged that comfortable accommodation was found for two recumbent figures upon the standard regulation army stretchers, these being supported on long, easy springs which ran from end to end. From the bottom springs a cradle passed across from one side to the other, at each side, and these were slotted to take the feet of the stretcher. Rubber blocks were fixed so that the wood of the stretcher did not rest upon the metal cradle. The upper springs had metal attachments which passed similarly from one side spring to the other, and these were made to swing around on a pivot so as to allow the bearer of the bottom stretcher to walk right through the sidecar. Tubular

stanchions were fitted at the five extreme corners of the framework, and these carried a waterproof cover.

Early in the war a radio telephone and telegraph set was devised by a New York inventor for use by armies on the march in the field. The equipment was contained in a metal sidecar attached to a motorcycle. The transmitting power was approximately one kilowatt with a resultant radius for the wireless telegraph of 80 to 100 miles and about half that distance for the radio telephone.

Current was supplied to the telephone or telegraph by a high voltage direct current generator connected directly to an independent motorcycle engine contained within the sidecar. The wireless equipment comprised a complete unit entirely independent of the motorcycle. It could be readily detached and pushed by hand or loaded upon a wagon and transported over rough ground. An extra wheel was provided which could be attached

Radio outfit in a sidecar (Scientific American, 3/27/15)

Field radio telegraph and telephone station using a motorcycle power plant (Scientific American, 3/27/15)

to either hub of the side car or to the front or rear of the motorcycle.

The antenna was supported by a light weight metal mast of tubular construction. The form was telescopic, so that the mast when collapsed could be easily strapped out of the way on the side of the car.

In 1915 Corporal Greenhow Johnston of Richmond, Virginia, organized a motorcycle squad of eight men for auxiliary service in the Signal Corps of the Virginia Volunteers. This group proved

Motorcycle squad and wireless apparatus of the signal corps, Virginia Volunteers (Scientific American, 2/26/16)

the military value of motorcycles by their exploits, especially in connection with portable wireless stations, which were carried with remarkable rapidity from point to point over roads little better than foot paths, and readily set up and operated.

The following is quoted from a report sent by Capt. F. S. Splatt, Type D Signal Corps, Virginia Volunteers, to the Adjutant General of Virginia, relative to the volunteer motorcycle squad:

In accordance with the policy outlined by the commander of the company, this command assembled 8 A.M., Nov. 7th, for mounted practice. 45 men and 1 officer reported. One wire cart, one wagon and two pack mules were used. The motorcycle squad recently organized in the company was used for the first time. The command left the armory 9 A.M., and proceeded to the

Standard wireless pack set of the United States Army, carried on a motorcycle side car (Scientific American, 2/26/16)

state fair grounds in regular formation. One ration was carried.

Equation exercises were given for about two hours, followed by section drill of about one hour's duration. Wire lines were laid within the fair grounds; communications were excellent. One radio station was erected at Byrd Park, several miles away, and one at headquarters (fair grounds). Communication was instantaneous and perfect. The radio pack sets are a success in every way.

I cannot speak too highly of the speed and efficiency of the motorcycle section; this branch of the work is really a side issue of signal corps work and has never been authorized by the War Department. The great speed over the pack mules, and the ability to get over the ground almost as well as the pack mules are the good features.

The expenses incident to the work by the motorcycle squad have been paid by the individual owners of these machines. The company commander approves that these owners should be reimbursed for fuel and wear and tear on the machines out of the funds allotted for practice drills.

I consider the practice drill a success, a great help to the organization.

The wireless sets used by the volunteer organization were of the standard U.S. Army pack type, equipped with a pole made in sections and a hand-driven generator. Practically no alterations were necessary in converting the standard motorcycle

fitted with a sidecar into a motorcycle wireless plant.

Other uses for the motorcycle mushroomed. It was just as dependable a vehicle as its larger brother, the automobile, and it provided a very economical means of transportation. Motorcycles with sidecars were common and the fitting of clutch control and change-speed gearing made it easy for the relatively low powered motorcycle engines to handle much heavier loads than seemed possible.

In 1917 a new attachment in the form of a rear car that had its own independent wheels and axle increased the load carrying capacity considerably. It attached to the motorcycle in much the same way that a wagon is hitched to a horse. As the tractive pull came in the center of the rear car, the machine did not tend to steer to one side as when a sidecar was attached, and the combination was easily controlled. The outfit illustrated was devised for military and police purposes and was known as a "riot car." Four men could easily be carried on the rear car and one on the motorcycle saddle. A substantial delivery box could be substituted for the seats, adapting the machine for commercial purposes. A special armored body with provisions for carrying a machine gun and two operatives was also devised by the makers for use in the army. The motorcycle could be detached in a few minutes and absolutely no change in its construction was needed to adapt it to pulling a rear car.

Motorcycle fitted with a "riot car" (Scientific American, 9/15/17)

Setting up the gun for operation on the ground (Scientific American, 8/4/17)

America noted the importance of motorcycle use in the war going on in Europe and began to brush up her own battalions. England alone had 30,000 machine guns mounted on motorcycles, finding them indispensable for work in sudden emergencies. Motorcycles were the fastest way to get machine guns to a point of attack, bring a sudden enfilade fire on an enemy trench, or to dislodge an observation or sniping post. Without machine guns no infantry could be considered adequately supported, and to make them effective they had to be as mobile as possible. In this work the automobile was not found to be as efficient as the motorcycle, as the lighter and more flexible machine could be quickly brought to positions unaccessible to the large cars and offered smaller targets for enemy gunfire.

Contrary to popular belief, the machine guns were seldom operated from their motor carriages for the reason these carriages did not afford a sufficiently rigid firing platform, and, moreover, when so operated, they offered altogether too conspicuous a target. It was customary to leave the motorcycle at a safe distance in the rear and then carry the gun forward to the desired location, where it was set up on a special tripod on the ground. Occasions had occurred where a machine gun battery had unexpectedly run into a picket or scouting party of the enemy, and of course the men had done the best they could by firing from the motor mount, but these were exceptional cases.

In earlier motorcycle machine-gun batteries the guns were mounted on tripods set on the sidecar platforms, but experience proved it was better to do away with this tripod and to strap the gun on the machine in the lowest position possible, as it was found that by thus lowering the center of gravity of the outfit it could be operated with greater speed over rough ground, and more effectively than when the gun was carried in the old way. If an emergency arose the men would have to depend on their automatic pistols for fighting, and these were con-

Utilizing a field of daisies as a screen for the machine-gun (Scientific American, 8/4/17)

A machine-gun as mounted on a side car (Scientific American, 8/4/17)

Motorcycle machine-gun battery (Scientific American, 8/4/17)

had to be good riders and operators, and so intimately acquainted with the mechanics of their machines that they could keep them constantly in good working order. They had to be able to make all ordinary repairs, for although in the armies of Europe, efficient repair stations were maintained at suitable points in the rear, it was not always convenient or possible to take a defective machine to the rear. While the machines had to be rushed at great speed over rough country, reckless driving was consistently discouraged because it resulted in unnecessary destruction of the motorcycles, and every effort was made to keep the battery at all times in a condition for instant service.

The heavy twin-cylinder machines so popular in America were not considered in Europe to be

sidered to be as effective under the conditions as the machine gun would be. The men seldom carried rifles.

The men in motorcycle machine-gun batteries

Close-up of one of the units (Scientific American, 8/4/17)

Inexperienced military motorcyclist has an accident
(Scientific American)

particularly well adapted for dispatch work, but they were eminently fitted for the work of transporting machine guns, and for this were probably better than any other motorcycle produced in the world. The rough roads of this country had tended to develop types and methods of construction that resulted in unusual strength and reliability, making them particularly suited to the heavy work of transporting machine guns over difficult country.

24

Bicycle Mania

AFTER WORLD WAR I THE INDUSTRIAL REVOLU-tion catapulted the world into mechanization. The heyday of the automobile arrived—first as a "flivver" and "tin Lizzie," and then on to greater achievements as the car grew bigger, more sophisticated, more of an insatiable gas guzzler. Bicycles were relegated to the children's department mostly, the exceptions being their use by people concerned with good health and exercise and those too poor to purchase an automobile.

Gradually, the knowledge came that oil supplies were limited. A stunned public sat in a long gas lines at filling stations, went through all sorts of odd/even-day buying, and always the threat of gas rationing hung over their heads. The big, comfortable, low-milage-per-gallon cars had seen their day. Once again the trend was toward smaller vehicles using less gas and people-powered vehicles using none at all. History was about to roll over and repeat itself.

In 1978 Americans bought more than 9 million bicycles according to estimates by the Bicycle Manufacturers Association—up from 6.2 million in 1967 and 7.3 million in 1975. Surveys indicate sales will increase to 11 million in 1980 and 19 million by 1990. It is estimated there are more than 90 million bicycles in use today.

Other wheeled vehicles enjoyed popularity, too. In 1978 *Time* featured a young man, John Buchan,

who daily roller-skated seven miles across San Francisco to his office to work, and considering the heavy traffic in this great city, only a brave man indeed would commute in this way.

The Bay City offered a roller-skating messenger service, which was no doubt faster than any winged Mercury. Grocery shoppers skated from store to store, mothers skated while pushing carriages ahead, and even the governor's lady skated to a luncheon date with him.

From the Golden Gate to New York's Central Park, skaters took over the nation's parkways. The new skates were unlike the old steel clamp-ons that kids once wore. They were light and slid smoothly over cracked surfaces with quiet grace, and of course, cost a great deal more. Customized ones went for $1,000 of more, so rental companies that charged about $2 per hour sprang up to supply the demand.

In Minneapolis the owner of a skating equipment store used skates for transportation. He said they were better than a bike because you didn't have to worry about locking them up when you got where you were going. He was not alone as the skating craze grew. The U.S. Amateur Confederation of Roller Skating listed 12,000 speed skaters, 17,000 artistic skaters and several thousand hockey skaters in their membership. Skating rinks revived to thriving attendance, and when the disco craze came in, it naturally followed there would be dancing on skates.

Inventors wracked their brains for ideas for skates, accessories, and a San Francisco man offered a "new" invention—a roller-skate brake—which was duly hailed in the papers. When the New York transit system went on strike in 1980, UPI published as news a businessman roller-skating to work.

In 1960 skateboards were introduced as children's toys and were so dangerous they were often banned. It was thought to be a passing madness, but the craze grew. From mere wheels nailed to boards, the vehicles became sophisticated roller-bearing speedsters costing a great deal of money. Parks were built especially for skateboarders, accessories of every kind offered, and their production brought manufacturers millions of dollars each year.

Velocipede mania returned, although nobody called bikes that any more. In 1973 Japan decreed that bicycles be used for transportation to dispel the problems of smog, fumes, traffic congestion—and to save energy. Their solution to one problem presented another when millions of men, women and children pedaled off to work, school, and on errands, and found there was no place to park their vehicles. They left them in streets, on sidewalks, and on top of one another in a hopeless maze. At last report, no solution had been found, but the smog had disappeared.

Europe experienced a bicycle boom, and in 1978 West Germany reported sales had topped more than 4 million, 1.8 million more than the number of newly registered cars the year before. Four in five of all households, and two in three of all citizens had a bicycle. The government in Bonn awakened to the potential of bicycles as a fairly fast, flexible, and everyday means of inner urban transport.

The inventors were always present. In 1978 a German engineer, Hans Gunter Bals, offered a bike that was ridden like a horse, as a new innovation. It looked like a conventional machine, but instead of pedaling up and down, the rider pressed both feet down at the same time. It was a shame he didn't make it look like a horse as the velocipede once did.

Mopeds came back, although they weren't powered by steam engines this time. These presented problems as well as solutions. They could go at least 30 miles per hour and travel 150 miles or so on a gallon of gas, but anyone could drive one because they were classed as bicycles and no license required. Not many statistics are available, but in France, 17 percent of traffic-related deaths were credited to the moped. Safety warnings were issued, but the daredevils are always with us.

Speedy little mopeds are powered by all sorts of devices. At the solar energy fair in Sasbach, West Germany, in 1978, a solarmobile was exhibited. The solar cells were mounted atop the tricycle like an umbrella and the vehicle could run as long as the sun shone. It was touted as being Europe's first solar-powered vehicle, but others were sure to follow.

Even leg-powered bikes gave trouble. Davis, California, offered the "first" bicycle cop to control the thousands of cyclists attending the university there. He went in hot pursuit of lawbreakers and issued tickets for such infractions as running stoplights, riding on sidewalks, and going the wrong way on a one-way street. Fines were levied in proportion to the crime.

Since 1972 more bicycles than automobiles have been sold in the United States. As a result, more bike lanes have been established, more roads taken over by bikers, and of course, today's bike riders were yesterday's car drivers and laws had to be modified accordingly.

The *Los Angeles Times* gave space to an article about a "new" buscycle in operation—bicycles were hung on the outside to be transported while their riders rode the bus. News? Of course it was—just as it had been a hundred years before.

Flyers still attempted to fly man-powered crafts, and unlike the old aviettes, this generation succeeded. On June 12, 1979, a world-heralded event took place. In response to a $200,000 offer by the London Royal Aeronautical Society for the first man-powered flight across the English Channel, Bryan Allen of Bakersfield, California, pedaled his way to fame.

His craft was the *Gossamer Albatross*, a fragile, translucent craft, designed by a Pasadena aeronauticist who was puzzled by how many previous attempts had failed to achieve flight on muscle power alone. Paul MacCready was the holder of a Ph.D. in aeronautics from Caltech and president of an engineering consultant firm called AeroVironment Inc., and he designed the *Gossamer* well. He had to, for there were at least twenty other teams with vehicles as esoteric, imaginative, and flimsy as the *Gossamer,* and all after the prize.

MacCready first got the idea in 1976 from hang gliders while he was on vacation. He could make an aircraft larger without making it heavier, and he knew that as speed lessens, so does the power requirement to overcome air resistance. A pair of well-conditioned human legs could put out about ½ horsepower for sustained periods, a hang glider needed from 1.2 to 1.5 horsepower to stay aloft, so if he could triple the dimensions of a glider without changing its weight, only about a third as much power would be needed to stay aloft.

The resulting aircraft didn't look much like a hang glider with its long squared-off wings, small control surface out front, and propeller in back, but it was big and light. The first version weighed only 55 pounds, but it went up to about 70 pounds when safety and communication devices were added. For weight reduction, the builders first wrapped aluminum in carbon fiber impregnated with epoxy glue, then left the wrapped tube in acid until all

that was left was the wrapping—an ultralight tube of carbon fiber. The use of Dupont's products enabled MacCready to get the giant firm to sponsor the flight across the English Channel and foot the bill for the entire crew. The team included experts in structural techniques, boating, flight operations, fabrication engineering, exercise physiology, navigation and slow-speed propeller design.

And so the inventive race goes on, only with newer and more sophisticated fields to conquer. Bicycles, skates, skateboards, mopeds, motorcycles—you name the type and there are magazines faithfully reporting each "new" invention and design as it is offered. As always, the patent office is inundated by applications as the inventors get into the competitive spirit of seeing who can present the best, the most unheard-of, the outlandish, the practical, the *needed* for human transportation. And if you listen closely, on the wind comes the chuckling sound of contented ancestors viewing the antics of their busy offspring.

Index